# Preparing for

# KOREAN UNIFICATION

## Scenarios & Implications

Jonathan D. Pollack

Chung Min Lee

Prepared for the United States Army

The Arroyo Center

RAND

# PREFACE

If and when Korean unification occurs, it will constitute one of the decisive strategic changes in Northeast Asia since the outbreak of the Korean conflict nearly half a century ago. Depending on how various political, military, economic, and regional factors come into play, the outcome of the unification process could range from relatively manageable endgames to highly problematic and violent ones. Managing the results of the unification process will also usher in major new challenges for the United States, the Republic of Korea (ROK), and the U.S. Army.

This report evaluates four alternative unification scenarios, each with corresponding characteristics, potential indicators, variations, and operational implications for the Army. We have labeled these scenarios according to their predominant characteristics: (1) integration and peaceful unification; (2) collapse and absorption; (3) unification through conflict; and (4) disequilibrium and potential external intervention. By describing the major dimensions of each scenario, we can identify some of the policy and operational challenges that U.S. and ROK security planners could face under each outcome.

The findings in this report summarize and integrate the results of a research project on "Korean Unification: Implications for the U.S. Army," sponsored by the Deputy Chief of Staff for Intelligence, U.S. Army, and conducted in RAND Arroyo Center's Strategy and Doctrine Program. The Arroyo Center is a federally funded research and development center sponsored by the United States Army.

# CONTENTS

# FIGURES

# TABLES

## THE LOOMING KOREAN CRISIS

Nearly a decade after the fall of the Soviet Union, the Korean peninsula remains the final Cold War frontier. South and North Korea are still in a technical state of war, with the military confrontation between the respective states constituting the most heavily armed face-off anywhere on the globe (1.1 million troops in the North and 680,000 in the South). The United States also continues to deploy nearly 40,000 military personnel in Korea for deterrence and defense. Given North Korea's ballistic missile, artillery, and chemical weapons capabilities, any outbreak of hostilities on the peninsula carries potentially catastrophic consequences, especially in view of Seoul's proximity to the demilitarized zone (DMZ) separating South and North.

Despite the seeming rigidity of the South-North relationship, inter-Korean dynamics could shift fundamentally over the next decade, and quite possibly much sooner. Preparing for this possibility will increasingly define U.S. Army roles and responsibilities on the peninsula. The proximate cause of this potential change is the growing economic and political vulnerability of the North Korean state, and the broad range of consequences this vulnerability could unleash. North Korea is largely bereft of its past alliance bonds with Russia and China, while simultaneously confronting unprecedented challenges to its long-term viability. With the North no longer able to rely on open-ended subsidies from Moscow and Beijing, its economic output has shrunk by more than half since 1990. The defining imperative of the North Korean state is no longer to present itself as an alternative model for Korean unification, but to avoid extinction as a political, economic, and social system: regime survival has superseded all other national goals.

Notwithstanding periodic military actions undertaken by the North against the South, peace has been maintained in Korea for four and a half decades. But North Korea's increasing vulnerabilities create a growing likelihood of major change, even over the near to middle term. Though it is impossible to predict with confidence the timing and precise dimensions of such change, it will entail major strategic and operational consequences for the United States, the Republic of Korea (ROK), and for the military forces of both countries. Thus, the "how" of major change—including the possibility that it could trigger abrupt movement toward unification—is at least as important as the "if" or "when."

To address these possibilities and their potential consequences, this study examines four alternative scenarios that could lead to Korean unification, and it assesses their strategic and operational implications. Each scenario has its own characteristics, and each would entail very different implications for the Army: (1) peaceful integration and unification; (2) collapse and unification through absorption; (3) unification through conflict; and (4) sustained disequilibrium with potential external intervention.

## THE CHANGING SECURITY ENVIRONMENT

The possibility of major political-military change in the North is the pivotal "strategic driver" of future security on the peninsula. Even as Pyongyang's economic performance has deteriorated profoundly over the past decade, the North has been able to exploit its growing weapons of mass destruction (WMD) capabilities for political and economic leverage and as a force multiplier. Although the likelihood of a major conventional conflict comparable to the Korean War has declined in recent years, the spectrum of conflict possibilities on the peninsula has expanded markedly, from WMD use on one end to military operations other than war (MOOTW) on the other.

The possibility of regime or even state collapse in North Korea has further redefined the defense planning assumptions of the United

States and the ROK.  It would no doubt be vastly preferable if a transformation in the North unfolded gradually and free of major violence or internal upheaval, enabling a step-by-step process of peninsular integration and diminished levels of military confrontation.  But the possibility of such a benign outcome seems highly remote.  Despite major new initiatives proffered by ROK President Kim Dae Jung and notwithstanding the North's grim economic circumstances, Pyongyang displays virtually no interest in a meaningful political accommodation with the South on equitable terms.

The possibility of future instability in North Korea and the enhanced prospect of unification have therefore compelled the United States and the ROK to redefine the purposes underlying their defense planning efforts.  Security planning must allow for far greater flexibility and adaptability than when the alliance focused almost exclusively on the "canonical threat" of an invasion by the North.  This variability and uncertainty requires a new, very different mix of Army capabilities.  The U.S. and ROK militaries also need to review their capabilities in relation to the prodigious challenges that would accompany the political, economic, social, and infrastructural rebuilding of the North.

The future of the Korean peninsula has been further complicated by the economic crisis that first enveloped much of East Asia in the summer of 1997, including the ROK.  Notwithstanding the economic and financial dimensions of these events for South Korea's long-term development, the security implications cannot be ignored.  Some of the ROK's force modernization goals have been delayed, and (depending on the pace of economic recovery) may need to be further reassessed.  South Korea's domestic economic preoccupations have also reinforced prevailing sentiment in the ROK to avoid any abrupt change in the North, given the prodigious costs and complexities of the unification process.  Regardless of President Kim Dae Jung's declaration that the ROK does not seek to absorb North Korea or to hasten unification, such policies could easily be overtaken by events.  The international community as a whole may be able to delay acute instability in the North, but such instability will very likely have a dynamic of its own, independent of the preferences and policies of others.  Thus, preparing for a wider range of possible outcomes (as envisioned under the four alternative scenarios) is an

increasing imperative for the United States and the ROK, as well as
other surrounding powers, especially China.

## NORTH KOREA'S UNCERTAIN FUTURE

Were it not for North Korea's military capabilities, the possibility of
regime or state collapse, and the peninsula's strategic location, this
state would receive only minimal international attention. Because of
these factors, North Korea's future evolution will fundamentally affect peninsular and regional security. But North Korea's prospects
and capabilities must be understood in terms of the country's internal dynamics and the decisions of its supreme leader, Kim Jong Il.
The extreme personalization of political power in the North will
largely determine North Korea's responses to four key policy challenges:

* Reversing the decline of an increasingly sclerotic command
  economy while continuing to spend close to 25 percent of a
  shrinking gross national product (GNP) on defense.

* Attempting to overcome acute structural problems in the economy without introducing major reforms that could erode central
  political control and trigger larger internal consequences, including internal challenges to the Kim Jong Il regime.

* Continuing to participate in bilateral and multilateral accords
  and negotiations (e.g., the October 1994 Agreed Framework, the
  Korean Peninsula Energy Development Organization, and the
  four-party talks), thereby garnering additional international assistance, while avoiding concessions that would undermine
  Pyongyang's larger diplomatic and military strategies.

* Maintaining its foreign policy opening with the United States
  while avoiding full-scale relations with South Korea that could
  undermine the North's national sovereignty and claims of legitimacy.

### Reversing North Korea's Economic Decline

The steady erosion of the North's economic capabilities looms as an
ever more pressing concern to its leadership. The Kim Jong Il regime
has three basic choices to reverse this decline. First, it can imple-

ment major economic reforms, beginning with the introduction of more market-oriented policies; second, it can permit piecemeal cosmetic changes, including the solicitation of foreign investment for special economic zones; and third, it can seek to "muddle through" by tactical economic adjustments and expectations of open-ended international provision of foodstuffs, energy, and various forms of humanitarian assistance. If the North Korean regime launched major market-oriented economic reforms, the country would very likely face massive socioeconomic disruption and a growing challenge to its political legitimacy. But if the leadership resists major change, the country's economic base will decline further, ultimately threatening the regime's viability. This is a dilemma for which the North Korean leadership has no long-term answer, though it will seek to delay a major reckoning as long as possible.

Pyongyang will in all likelihood pursue a "muddling through" strategy for the present, since this could yield critical infusions of external assistance (including from the ROK and the United States) without requiring major internal changes. But this alternative cannot be considered a long-term solution. However, a larger shift in economic policy would entail substantial political risks to the Kim Jong Il regime, since Kim's political legitimacy rests on fealty to long-entrenched autarkic strategies established by his father, Kim Il Sung.

Absent an appreciable economic recovery, the regime's longer-term prospects seem increasingly grim. This progressive decline can be characterized as a descending spiral in which the North's prospects for survival steadily narrow through six potential stages:

- Economic and political atrophy;
- Economic breakdown;
- Political instability;
- Regime breakdown;
- Regime and/or state collapse;
- Conflict or absorption.

The first three stages constitute characteristics of overall strategic decay, whereas the second three stages are manifestations of accelerated strategic decay. North Korea today is between the first two stages (atrophy and economic breakdown).  Though accelerated decay does not appear imminent, it cannot be ruled out in the near to middle term.  However, since these latter stages would indicate a major degradation of the regime's political and internal security mechanisms rather than a further deterioration of the system's economic performance as such, it is possible that a weakened North could somehow persist, albeit not indefinitely.

Despite ongoing efforts by the outside world to arrest North Korea's economic decline—including the large-scale provision of energy, food, and humanitarian assistance and modest increases in North Korea's external trade relations—it is highly unlikely that the current regime will undertake major reform of its own accord.  In the final analysis, the status quo in North Korea cannot be maintained indefinitely, with a heightening of internal contradictions ultimately undermining regime stability and viability.

## THE ROLE OF CHINA

Despite the above forecast, unification is not inevitable.  If the regime is somehow able to sustain itself over the next decade and engineer at least a modest economic recovery, the stalemate between the two Koreas could be prolonged indefinitely.  The role of outside powers, especially China, would be pivotal in this scenario. If China decides to substantially augment its assistance to the North, the regime's chances for survival would be considerably enhanced. Though the Chinese have increased their energy and food aid in recent years, leaders in Beijing seem disinclined to undertake heroic measures on behalf of the North.  But there appear to be three circumstances under which the Chinese might weigh such a course of action:  (1) if the North (despite a clear aversion to dependence on China) signals its readiness to "tilt" toward Beijing in exchange for enhanced economic and political support; (2) if the indicators of instability in the North and its repercussions for stability and security in contiguous border areas convince the Chinese that they need to act to manage the risks to their security and ensure their long-term interests; or (3) if the ROK and the United States embark on unilateral actions to counter instability in the North that China believes would undermine its long-term political and security interests.

However, the prospect of such major shifts in Chinese policy still seems unlikely. Should the signs of an impending crisis in the North begin to mount, Beijing might well opt to heighten its consultations with Washington and with Seoul, even as China also enhances its capacity to act unilaterally. The Chinese clearly retain a substantial capability to shape longer-term peninsular outcomes. This factor warrants careful assessment by the United States and ROK, especially if shifts in Chinese policy toward the North become more evident. But such possibilities underscore the additional need for much closer consultations among the United States, ROK, and China.

## IMPLICATIONS FOR THE U.S. ARMY

Of the four scenarios analyzed in this study, the Army is most familiar with the conflict scenario, since it has continuously and actively prepared for major theater war for decades. But future developments in North Korea could result in outcomes that depart substantially from a full-scale attack on the ROK, as noted below.

### Flexible Roles and Missions

The Army needs to prepare for a much wider range of roles and missions with limited warning, in more compressed time frames, and under new operational conditions that could diverge from well-established policies and practices. In the event of an abrupt North Korean collapse, U.S. Army and ROK army units attached to the Combined Forces Command (CFC) would have to perform a very different range of missions. Among them are humanitarian assistance, various types of peace operations, dismantling and management of weapons of mass destruction (WMD), and the demobilization of the North Korean armed forces. If instability persists in North Korea but without collapse, the Army will need to enhance its present deterrent options and augment its extant capabilities, given that a weakened but more unstable North would remain an ongoing concern for ROK and U.S. security planners.

## New Intelligence Demands

The Army also needs to enhance its intelligence-collection and analysis capabilities.  The demand for timely intelligence will increase appreciably if North Korea appears on the brink of a collapse, or if China seems poised to take actions, including a major augmentation of economic and humanitarian assistance and redeployments of selected military units toward the Chinese–North Korean border.  If the Kim Jong Il regime is replaced by a party-military junta, Army intelligence would face the task of analyzing the overall military capabilities of the new regime, its levels of military preparedness, and the extent and effectiveness of central control over North Korean military assets, especially control of WMD assets.  In addition, data collection and assessment of Chinese–North Korean political, military, and economic relations would loom as a major challenge.  Even under current circumstances, these issues all represent pressing analytic and intelligence priorities.

## Operational Requirements

The Army will also face new operational requirements as Korea moves toward unification, in particular should the reconstruction of the North's economy and infrastructure and the peninsula's integration into a single political entity become a reality.  These circumstances will raise unprecedented and extremely complex problems, requiring a mix of Army capabilities very different from the present one.  Operational control arrangements will necessitate new guidelines for CFC and non-CFC operations, including new rules of engagement and new logistical requirements.  Dismantling North Korea's WMD arsenal could result in new missions for the U.S. Army and could be undertaken bilaterally (with the ROK) or multilaterally.  New command and control procedures may need to be devised with ROK forces, depending on the nature of the operational demands that arise during the unification process.

All the above challenges highlight the need for the Army to be prepared for a much wider array of contingencies—even as these contingencies remain subject to substantial uncertainty.

# ACKNOWLEDGMENTS

This study originated in the strong interest expressed by the Office of the Deputy Chief of Staff for Intelligence (DCSINT) to undertake an independent assessment of various "what if" scenarios for Korea that could develop under conditions of dynamic change. The authors are especially indebted to Colonel William Speer and Charles Jones for their encouragement and timely support. Other individuals in both the U.S. and Korean governments generously shared their time and insights.

We were also much stimulated by discussions with Thomas McNaugher, then Director of the Arroyo Center's Strategy and Doctrine Program, who strongly supported this endeavor from its outset. His active encouragement was crucial in shaping the design and directions of the project as a whole. David Kassing and Thomas Szayna subsequently provided much-needed support, in particular as we sought to "translate" various project briefings into a written document. Other RAND colleagues, especially Robert Howe, provided timely assistance at different stages of the project. The copious editorial suggestions of Judy Larson and Nikki Shacklett warrant special thanks.

The authors also wish to acknowledge the detailed and very constructive technical reviews provided by Bruce Bennett and Paul Bracken.

RAND *MR1040-1*

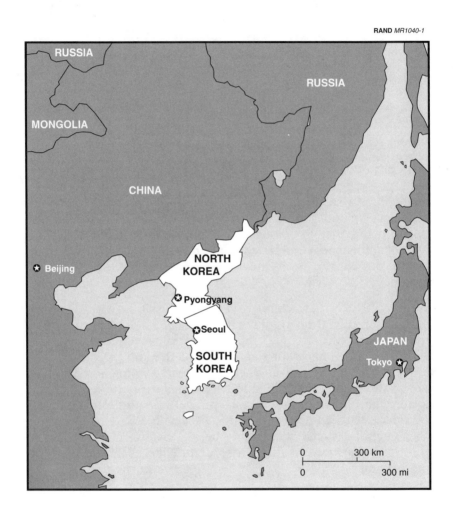

**Korea and Northeast Asia**

# Chapter One

# INTRODUCTION

For half a century, the world has grown accustomed to a divided Korea. More than forty-five years after the end of the Korean conflict, the North and the South remain in a technical state of war, with the military confrontation between the two states the most heavily armed face-off in the world (1.1 million troops in the North and 680,000 troops in the South). In addition, the United States continues to deploy nearly 40,000 military personnel in Korea for deterrence and defense. Given North Korea's arsenal of ballistic missiles, long-range artillery, and chemical weapons, any outbreak of hostilities on the peninsula is potentially catastrophic, especially in view of Seoul's proximity to the demilitarized zone (DMZ) separating South and North.

From the outside looking in, the Korean peninsula seems frozen in time. Yet despite this seeming rigidity, inter-Korean dynamics, driven particularly by internal changes in the North, could create a fundamental transformation on the Korean peninsula in the coming decade, and quite possibly much sooner. The proximate cause of this potential change is the increasing economic and political vulnerability of the North Korean state, which finds itself largely bereft of its past alliance bonds with Russia and China and confronting prodigious challenges to its longer-term viability.

North Korea's defining imperative is no longer to present itself as an alternative model for Korean unification, but to arrest its internal decline and avoid extinction as a political, economic, and social system: state survival has superseded all other national goals. To be sure, a sharp alteration of the status quo, including regime collapse or systemic implosion, cannot be predicted with certainty; such change might occur with little or no warning. But defense planners can no longer rule out such possibilities. If there is a major rupture in the North Korean system in the not-too-distant future, it will have crucial strategic and operational consequences for the United States, the Republic of Korea (ROK), and the military forces of both countries. It is therefore essential that we understand fully the sources of potential instability in North Korea; possible indicators of this instability; the various forms or paths that such change could take; and its implications for U.S. and ROK defense planning, with particular attention to the consequences for the U.S. Army.

## THE CHANGING PENINSULAR SECURITY ENVIRONMENT

Since the end of the Korean War in 1953, the United States and South Korea have shared two central strategic objectives: prevent the outbreak of another major conflict and, should deterrence fail, defend the territorial and political integrity of the Republic of Korea. At the same time, the two allies have also stressed the central importance of peaceful change on the Korean peninsula that could eventually lead to the creation of a democratic, unified Korean state. But the strategic and operational implications of Korean unification were not fully acknowledged until the unification of Germany in October 1990 and the dissolution of the Soviet Union at the end of 1991.

North Korea at present poses a different type of military threat than it did during much of the Cold War, as evinced by Pyongyang's increased exploitation of weapons of mass destruction (WMD) as a source of political and economic leverage and as a key force multiplier. Although the possibility of a full-scale conventional war can never be ruled out, that particular military threat has diminished appreciably since the late 1980s. Russia (though it has initialed a new bilateral treaty with North Korea) is no longer committed to automatic military involvement in a crisis, and China (though still nominally allied with Pyongyang) has conveyed that it is not prepared to come to North Korea's defense should Pyongyang launch an unprovoked attack on the ROK. Though Russian and Chinese behavior might prove different in a crisis, these policy declarations bespeak an appreciably diminished political and security relationship between Pyongyang and its erstwhile allies.

In part to compensate for the loss of this support, North Korea has sought to broaden its strategic options through a robust ballistic missile program, a chemical and biological weapons capability, and most important, retention of a nuclear weapons option.[1]  But eight successive years of economic decline, acute food shortages in certain regions of the North, precipitous drops in industrial production, and aging weapon systems have resulted in a relative and absolute diminution in North Korean economic capacities and military readiness.[2]  ROK government estimates nonetheless assert that North Korea continues to allocate close to 25 percent of its shrinking GNP to military expenditure, and that the number of people serving in the armed forces has remained largely constant and may even have increased on the margins.[3]  Major fuel shortages, reduced defense industrial output, limitations on spare parts availability, and noncombat military assignments undertaken by the Korean People's Army (KPA) have almost certainly impinged on war preparations. But it is impossible to estimate accurately how much combat capabilities as a whole have degraded.

In the context of these circumstances, the U.S.-ROK Combined Forces Command (CFC) continues to plan for a full range of contingencies on the peninsula, including major theater war. This multiplicity of defense plans reflects the expansion of the military threat spectrum on the peninsula since the end of the Cold War. For example, though the near-term nuclear threat was contained through the U.S.–North Korean Agreed Framework accord of October 1994, there is no assurance that North Korea has ceased work on a clandestine program, or that it does not retain a capability to resume such activities. North Korea continues to make periodic threats to restart its nuclear weapons program (in part, no doubt, to elicit further eco-

---

[1]For a succinct treatment of this issue, see Paul Bracken, "Risks and Promises in the Two Koreas," *Orbis,* Vol. 39, No. 1, Winter 1995, pp. 55–64.

[2]For a detailed assessment of North Korea's economic decline, consult Marcus Noland, Sherman Robinson, and Tao Wang, *Rigorous Speculation: The Collapse and Revival of the North Korean Economy* (Washington, D.C.: Institute for International Economics, Working Paper 99-1, 1999).

[3]*Defense White Paper, 1997–1998* (Seoul: The Ministry of National Defense, Republic of Korea, 1998), pp. 55–56.

nomic and energy assistance from the United States and others).[4] Other indications suggest that nuclear weapons development could be resumed at a major underground site under construction at Kumchang-ri, though visits by U.S. inspectors to the suspect site should enable the United States to clarify and monitor any activities under way at this location.[5]

In a major political-military crisis, U.S. and ROK response options could be constrained, perhaps severely, if North Korea threatens the use of nuclear weapons or other less lethal but more credible military capabilities (e.g., chemical weapons). In addition, as will be discussed below, accelerated political and economic instability in North Korea could trigger substantial internal dislocation with external consequences (for example, large-scale refugee flows into China and the ROK), or it could result in enhanced irregular warfare operations against South Korea. Military operations other than war (MOOTW) may increase in parallel with growing fears in Pyongyang of an inexorable shift in the "correlation of forces" in Seoul's favor, given the privation and decline that the North has been unable to reverse.

Thus, the increasing possibility of regime or even state collapse in North Korea has dramatically altered the larger context of U.S. and ROK defense planning. Nearly eight years after the dissolution of the Soviet Union and the beginning of North Korea's acute economic crisis, and nearly five years after the death of long-time leader Kim Il Sung, the Democratic People's Republic of Korea (DPRK) remains

---

[4]Elisabeth Rosenthal, "North Korea Says It Will Unseal Reactor," *The New York Times,* May 13, 1998; Kevin Sullivan,"North Korea Threatens Revival of Its Nuclear Program," *Washington Post,* May 15, 1998.

[5]According to congressional testimony of General John Tilelli, Jr., Commander in Chief of the Combined Forces Command and of United States Forces Korea, the intelligence community judges the Kumchang-ri construction effort "large enough to house a plutonium production facility and possibly a reprocessing plant." Although the project remains years from completion, General Tilelli expressed "deep concern that the North is continuing a covert nuclear weapons program." Statement of General John H. Tilelli, Jr., to the House National Security Committee, March 3, 1999. In mid-March 1999, the United States and North Korea reached an agreement allowing U.S. inspectors access to the suspect site, with the initial inspection in May 1999. David E. Sanger, "U.S. Aides in Pact with North Korea on a Suspect Site," *The New York Times,* March 17, 1999.

politically intact.[6] Indeed, the elevation of Kim Jong Il—Kim Il Sung's son and designated successor—to leading positions in the party, state, and military hierarchies suggests both the full consolidation of his personal power and the absence of any immediate challenge to his political dominance.[7]

However, Pyongyang's deteriorating economic and strategic fortunes over the past decade suggest that the status quo in North Korea will ultimately prove unsustainable. Over time, some systemic disruption or challenge at either the regime or state level appears increasingly likely. There seems little historical precedent for an economy to undergo such profound contraction without widespread political and societal effects. This is not to predict the precise conditions and circumstances that could produce major change. Indeed, North Korea's capacity to survive over the decades (and especially in the 1990s) attests to a durability and resiliency that continues to confound numerous political and strategic observers.[8] It seems clear that leadership cohesion has proved central to maintaining the viability of the state; various "collapse scenarios" are therefore more appropriately viewed in political rather than economic terms. However, absent a level of sustained external support and an ability to exploit the opportunities afforded by international food, energy, and humanitarian assistance, North Korea appears unlikely to be able to indefinitely defy political and economic laws of gravity.

Many analysts, however, assert that beneath North Korea's seeming rigidity and reiteration of military threats against the South, the outlines of a more flexible if not fully accommodative policy can be discerned. Much of this change has been manifest in Pyongyang's dealings with the United States, since the North's leadership believes that an upgraded relationship with Washington holds the key to enhancing international aid and assistance flows. Such assumptions also appear to underlie many of the major changes in ROK strategy

---

[6]For a careful analysis of North Korea's current circumstances and future prospects, consult David Reese, *The Prospects for North Korea's Survival* (London: International Institute for Strategic Studies, Adelphi Paper 323, November 1998).

[7]"Kim Jong Il Era Dawns, with Military's Stakes Enhanced," *Vantage Point*, Vol. 21, No. 9, September 1998, pp. 1–5.

[8]For a discerning discussion, see Norman D. Levin, "What If North Korea Survives?" *Survival*, Vol. 39, No. 4, Winter 1997–98, pp. 156–174.

toward the North initiated by President Kim Dae Jung, who (unlike his predecessor, Kim Young Sam) has vigorously pursued closer ties with Pyongyang, independent of whether these steps yield near-term political breakthroughs in South-North relations. The Agreed Framework accords, the U.S. brokering of follow-on arrangements for provision of two light-water nuclear reactors to the North under the terms of the Korean Peninsula Energy Development Organization (KEDO) agreement, and the agreement over access to the North Korean suspect site at Kumchang-ri are cited as relevant examples of such a strategy.

However, mounting concerns over North Korean compliance with the earlier nuclear accords as well as its accelerated missile development prompted a major review of U.S. policy toward the North, led by former Secretary of Defense William Perry. Should the North definitively halt its WMD and ballistic missile development and dismantle those capabilities deemed destabilizing to international security, a larger political-military transformation on the peninsula would seem possible, though far from fully assured. Over the longer run, the United States hopes that negotiated understandings with the North will yield important benefits: larger policy breakthroughs (including movement toward a peace treaty) in the four-party talks involving the United States, China, and the two Koreas; implementation of provisions of the 1991 Basic Agreement, including routinized high-level South-North meetings; mutually verifiable arms control and force reduction measures; visits between separated families; and fuller economic and institutional ties between South and North.

A central premise of several earlier reviews of U.S. policy toward North Korea was that an engagement strategy—by providing the North's leadership with clear incentives to collaborate with the outside world and by forestalling any potential near-term internal crisis—would enable Pyongyang to emerge as a more constructive actor, while also constraining activities overtly threatening to the security interests of the United States, ROK, and others (e.g., ballistic missile development and enhancement of WMD programs). Engagement would also facilitate reform policies and a more open attitude toward the outside world, with both sets of changes ultimately facilitating a nonantagonistic policy between the two Koreas. This latter step, in turn, might pave the way for a longer-term transition on the peninsula that moves toward integration and, ultimately, some form of political confederation, if not necessarily full unification.[9]

Such thinking also appears to underlie the prevailing lines of policy articulated by Kim Dae Jung. In his February 1998 inaugural address, President Kim put forward three basic principles that would govern the promotion of "peace, reconciliation, and cooperation" in South-North relations: (1) "no armed provocation by North Korea will be tolerated"; (2) "a takeover or absorption of North Korea will not be attempted"; and (3) "reconciliation and cooperation will be expanded."[10] The corollaries of these policies include the separation of politics from economics (thereby encouraging private enterprises to expand economic cooperation with the North, subject to government approval); enhanced contacts and visits by ROK citizens to the North; reciprocity and mutual accommodation between the two Korean governments; augmented food and humanitarian assistance to the North; and implementation of the ROK's commitments under the KEDO agreements. Despite subsequent North Korean actions that have contravened both the letter and spirit of these policies (notably, clandestine submarine operations in South Korean waters, continued ideological hostility directed against the ROK, further ballistic missile development, and evidence of a possible resumption of covert nuclear weapons development), President Kim has continued to reiterate his policies, encapsulated under what he describes as a "sunshine policy" toward the North. In addition, President Kim has urged the United States to lift many of its long-standing economic sanctions against the North.[11]

The pivotal assumption governing the reformulation of ROK strategy toward the North mirrors what one finds in various independent policy reviews: the belief that, over the longer run, North Korea will have no alternative but to undertake reform and accommodation

---

[9]For one of the fullest examinations of such an engagement strategy, see the June 1998 report of a Council on Foreign Relations Task Force, *Managing Change on the Korean Peninsula* (New York: Council on Foreign Relations, 1998).

[10]For an official exposition of these policies, see *The North Korea Policy of the Kim Dae Jung Administration* (Seoul: Ministry of Unification, Republic of Korea, 1998).

[11]See, for example, President Kim's February 1999 comments in an interview with an American journalist. Valerie Reitman, "'Positive' Signs from North Korea Cited," *Los Angeles Times*, February 13, 1999.

with the South, lest the system prove unable to sustain itself. In the words of the Council on Foreign Relations report, "[I]t is clear that Pyongyang has lost the competition between the two Koreas. Though the North remains stubbornly resistant to change and the opening of its system, *reform is now its only escape from continued erosion and eventual collapse.*"[12] By this logic, an incremental transition in the North will enable the regime to avoid extinction, ultimately permitting a meaningful, longer-term process of reconciliation with the South. Though the authors of this report acknowledge that North Korea might somehow continue to "muddle through," they assert that the latent possibility of instability now looms; in their view, more active policy measures must therefore be pursued in earnest to reduce the possibilities of internal upheaval.

In our judgment, this assessment slights several fundamental issues. Despite the evident flexibility and opportunity presented the North under the terms of Kim Dae Jung's initiatives, leaders in Pyongyang apparently find the "sunshine policy" more of a threat to the viability of their regime than the former, overtly hostile ROK policy. (However, this does not preclude the North from taking advantage of the sunshine policy's less-threatening components, in particular its commitment to enhanced economic and humanitarian assistance.) But North Korea views a breakthrough with the United States as pivotal to its longer-term political goals. Though the North has proposed political negotiations with the South, they are contingent on unilateral concessions by the ROK government that are transparently intended to undermine U.S.-ROK alliance ties.[13] An antagonistic policy toward the ROK is still an essential component of the North's insistence that it and not the South has legitimacy as a state. Viewed in this context, an internal reform process and a measure of South-North accommodation could accelerate rather than forestall state collapse. Indeed, authoritative statements in North Korean media draw precisely such a conclusion. In the aftermath of Kim Jong Il's

---

[12]*Managing Change on the Korean Peninsula*, p. 5. Emphasis added.

[13]Senior North Korean officials make no effort to conceal this intention. See, in particular, the speech by Kim Yong-sun, Secretary of the Korean Workers' Party Central Committee, February 3, 1999, in BBC *Selected World Broadcasts—Far East*, No. 3452, February 6, 1999, pp. D1–D4.

accession to supreme state power (paralleling his position in the military and party hierarchies), a major party editorial observed:

> The imperialists cry out for "reform" and "opening" with all the perpetuity of a Buddhist chant, but reform and opening are poisons. We have ceaselessly managed and improved our economy our own way, based on the principles of *juche* ideology, and we continue to make improvements. At this late date, we will not reform anew and we will not open.[14]

Thus, even as the editorial also conceded that "it is a fact that our socialist economy remains in crisis," prevailing policy continues to insist that North Korea must maintain its present course of action, lest an open door from South to North lead inexorably to an erosion of central control and, ultimately, to the end of the Kim Jong Il regime.

The North Korean leadership also recognizes that there is leverage in its acute economic vulnerabilities and pervasive shortages of energy, food, and related essentials. International support for various forms of aid that seek to prevent a major humanitarian crisis in the North has increased markedly, helping to compensate Pyongyang for the loss of external assistance at "friendship prices," especially the aid long proffered by the Soviet Union. (China remains a substantial aid donor to the North, although this assistance diminished sharply in the early 1990s. It has again increased in the latter half of the 1990s, but in aggregate terms has not reached levels comparable to assistance provided in the heyday of the Sino-Soviet rivalry. Moreover, a significant portion of Chinese assistance is no longer provided *gratis*.) An "aid-based" foreign policy strategy may be judged essential to North Korea's prospects for near- to mid-term survival, especially with respect to provision of energy supplies and foodstuffs.[15] In essence, such a life-support strategy—which the ROK government

---

[14]"Let Us Maintain Our Policy of Building a Self-Reliant People's Economy," *Nodong Sinmun* and *Kulloja* Joint Editorial, September 17, 1998, as reported in *Chosun Ilbo* on-line, September 18, 1998.

[15]For two suggestive assessments, see Philip Wonhyak Lim, "North Korea's Food Crisis," *Korea and World Affairs*, Vol. 21, No. 4, Winter 1997, pp. 568–585; and Nicholas Eberstadt, "North Korea's Interlocked Economic Crisis: Some Indications from 'Mirror Statistics,'" *Asian Survey*, Vol. 38, No. 3, March 1998, pp. 203–230.

estimates totaled nearly $1 billion between 1995 and 1998—has provided crucial infusions of aid to the North Korean regime, saving the leadership from having to make larger adaptations in its domestic or external strategies.[16] Indeed, such calculations have also been abundantly evident in the negotiations over U.S. access to the suspect site at Kumchang-ri. The March 1999 agreement, for example, stipulated that (in return for access to the site) North Korea will receive 600,000 tons of grain from the United States and various nongovernmental organizations.

Despite the North's capacity to turn such negotiating opportunities to advantage, the United States and the ROK have concluded that buying time—assuming that Pyongyang is unable to augment its threat to the South or to weaken U.S.-ROK alliance bonds—serves the interests of both countries. At the same time, the ROK's stated policy of nonabsorption can be viewed as a means to reassure the North about the South's intentions, irrespective of whether leaders in Pyongyang believe such statements to be credible. Though measures facilitating stabilization and incremental change are no doubt desirable, an effective policy cannot be based on an expectation that such a preferred outcome is assured. Indeed, in view of prevailing estimates about the vulnerabilities and uncertainties confronting the North, it seems highly doubtful that external aid—short of open-ended assistance on a scale that seems wholly unrealistic—can either rescue or resuscitate North Korea. This is not an argument contesting legitimate humanitarian assistance to the North, nor is it a proposal to somehow "hasten unification." But it seems crucial to identify some of the larger assumptions and limitations underlying current policy.

Thus, even though a gradualist, peaceful accommodation between the South and North is demonstrably preferable to any other outcome, we do not find it either likely or realistic. In contrast to his predecessor, President Kim Dae Jung asserts that the South has no intention of absorbing the North or of hastening its collapse, and he asserts that there is no realistic alternative to a strategy of engage-

---

[16]The Unification Ministry estimates the total assistance between 1995 and 1998 from the United States, ROK, United Nations, and various nongovernmental organizations (NGOs) to be $950.98 million. "North Korea Receives $950 Million in International Aid," *Korea Times,* October 7, 1998.

ment with the North, despite its manifest hostility to the ROK's initiatives. Indeed, President Kim has urged the United States to undertake major initiatives toward Pyongyang, even in the absence of appreciable breakthroughs between South and North. President Kim's
declarations, though reflecting an understandable desire to break
free from decades of confrontation and hostility on the peninsula,
are designed both to distinguish his efforts from longstanding ROK
policy and to cushion the potential for large-scale instability on the
peninsula.

The principal assumptions underlying long-term policy planning,
therefore, are relatively straightforward:

- The likelihood of gradual, peaceful accommodation between the
  two Koreas has always been exceedingly remote.

- The slogan of "peaceful unification" could be upheld on a largely
  cost-free basis so long as both regimes were viable political entities, but this assumption is increasingly problematic, given the
  North's mounting vulnerabilities.

- The internal decline in the North has substantially increased the
  possibility of major destabilizing change, though it remains
  impossible to predict when, where, and how such change will
  transpire.

- The North's leadership also continues to believe that enhancing
  its military threats against the South is vital to regime survival,
  even as these policies increase the risks of a highly destructive
  military conflict.

- It is therefore imperative that U.S. and ROK planning and actions
  be increasingly geared to preparing for such possibilities, and for
  mitigating their more extreme consequences.

Though an unconditional ROK olive branch to the North seemingly
creates an opportunity for major change, it would be exceedingly
imprudent to base longer-term policy on the expectation of meaningful reciprocation from leaders in Pyongyang. The fundamental
factors that explain mounting concerns about potential North
Korean instability stem from its internal condition, not the scope and
character of external assistance or the ROK's assurances of its benign
intentions. The basic issues for military planning seem clear-cut: if

and when instability occurs in the North, what should the United States and South Korea do to limit or manage the potential consequences?  What can be done now to prepare for such possibilities?  There may be an additional strategic goal of facilitating meaningful change in the North, but this cannot be the predominant objective of U.S. or ROK defense planning.  The increased possibility of instability in the North, even as Pyongyang retains an ample capability to inflict major damage on the ROK's economy and society, thus represents a very different and potentially even more demanding challenge for the U.S.-ROK military alliance.

## THE ROLES OF JAPAN, CHINA, AND RUSSIA

The possibility of destabilizing change in the North is increasingly (if implicitly) recognized by Japan, China, and Russia, the other major powers with major strategic interests on the Korean peninsula.  All three states are prudently if quietly repositioning their national strategies and policies, including increased attention to crisis-management requirements as well as planning for longer-term peninsular dynamics.  Tokyo, Beijing, and Moscow all offer lip service to the goal of unification, but it is doubtful that any are eager for it.  Each tacitly concurs with the predominant goals of U.S. policy on the peninsula (i.e., deterrence and defense, preventing WMD proliferation, and avoiding an acute humanitarian crisis or abrupt collapse).  In the near to middle term, each shares a common interest in maintaining stability, as seen from their separate vantage points.  But the interests and potential response options of all three powers vary considerably, and warrant separate discussion.

As a cornerstone U.S. ally in Northeast Asia, Japan could play a crucial role in a major peninsular crisis.  The Japanese are clearly worried about the implications of pronounced instability on the peninsula, but they are also acutely concerned about the security implications of North Korean missile development.  The three-stage Taepodong-1 missile launched on August 31, 1998, ostensibly in an effort to place a North Korean satellite in orbit, directly overflew Japanese territory, underscoring Pyongyang's ability to put Japanese targets at risk in the event of a future crisis on the peninsula.  The missile launch spurred support within Japan for more active exploration of theater missile defense (TMD) options, and it reinforced

Tokyo's incentives to remain closely aligned with the United States, no matter what the outcome on the peninsula.

At the same time, however, Japan remains highly constrained in its potential crisis-response options: there are continued constitutional inhibitions on Japan's right to assert collective defense responsibilities; its legal framework remains disconcertingly vague about the procedures and policies that would govern its conduct in a crisis; and there is no satisfactory national security mechanism and planning process. An equally important factor is Japan's history of occupation and colonialism in Korea, underscoring profound sensitivities within Korea concerning overt Japanese involvement in any future crisis as well as ample skittishness from the Japanese. For all these reasons, Japan has been largely content to follow rather than lead with respect to planning for peninsular instability, though Tokyo has been far less restrained in its expressed worries about accelerated North Korean missile development. The longstanding lack of a more comprehensive Japanese approach to peninsular stability left a major potential policy void that recent actions (notably, enhanced policy coordination with the United States and the ROK) have only begun to address.[17]

The inescapable reality is that Japan could readily find itself drawn into a future Korean crisis, though not in a direct combat role. In a range of scenarios, internal developments in the North could have pronounced spillover consequences—for example, a major humanitarian or refugee crisis; the need for noncombatant evacuation operations (NEO) of Japanese nationals resident on the peninsula; logistics and related support functions for U.S. forces in Japan; and U.S. use of Japanese bases in a crisis. These considerations have all been raised in deliberations over revisions of the U.S.-Japan Defense Guidelines and in U.S. encouragement for a heightened ROK-Japanese bilateral defense dialogue. Thus, despite Japan's clear-cut incentives and preferences for stabilization and gradual transition paths in the North,[18] there is a demonstrable need to prepare more

---

[17]For a forthright critique of Tokyo's previous policy (or nonpolicy) by a leading Japanese defense analyst, see Hideshi Takesada, "Scenarios for the Peninsula," *By the Way*, August–September 1996, pp. 18–23.

[18]Christopher W. Hughes, "Japanese Policy and the North Korean 'Soft Landing,'" *The Pacific Review*, Vol. 11, No. 3, 1998, pp. 389–415.

fully for an array of internal scenarios in the North with potential repercussions for Japan. A major crisis on the peninsula therefore represents one of the touchstone contingencies underlying U.S.-Japan alliance relations and internal security debate within Japan.

Chinese interests on the peninsula, while having some similarities with those in Japan, place it in a potentially even more pivotal position. Like Tokyo, Beijing has a predominant interest in sustaining the status quo, with most Chinese observers uneasy about the prospect of rapid unification. Unlike Tokyo, the Chinese maintain substantial equities with both Koreas, and if the peninsula unifies, they would immediately encounter substantial political and security consequences. Though Chinese specialists on Korea have long insisted that U.S. analysts have overstated the possibilities of upheaval in the North, since the mid-1990s there has been a pronounced if quiet change in Beijing's emphasis and tone with respect to peninsular futures. On the one hand, the Chinese have begun to acknowledge (albeit circumspectly) signs of instability in the North, and their economic support to Pyongyang (primarily in terms of grain supplies and crude oil) has increased from its lower levels during the first half of the decade. Moreover, Beijing and Pyongyang both make explicit reference to this assistance.[19] Some Chinese analysts voice (also quietly) increased worry about North Korean WMD activities, though nearly all public statements remain unusually circumspect. Indeed, Chinese statements assert that the United States and Japan are using the "pretext" of the North Korean missile test as a justification for enhancing TMD development.

At the same time, even as China has steadily expanded its economic and political ties with the ROK (two-way trade at present approaches $25 billion, with China now the ROK's third largest trading partner), Chinese wariness persists over various Seoul-centered unification scenarios and the U.S. role that might be entailed under various circumstances. Given that China's links to both Koreas (despite an

---

[19]See, for example, Xinhua, October 15, 1998, in BBC *Selected World Broadcasts—Far East*, No. 3366, October 29, 1998, p. D6. According to a Chinese military analyst, China's *gratis* assistance to the North in 1998 included 100,000 tons of grain, 20,000 tons of chemical fertilizers, and 80,000 tons of crude oil. Zhang Jinbao, "An Important Year in the Development of the Situation on the Korean Peninsula in 1998," *International Strategic Studies*, No. 1, 1999, p. 41. Aggregate Chinese assistance levels to the North are in all likelihood much higher.

increasing policy "tilt" in favor of the ROK) afford it substantial leverage in relation to future outcomes on the peninsula, there is still
ample uncertainty and evident internal debate over its preferred
strategy under more stressful circumstances.

Thus, future Chinese behavior (i.e., Beijing's incentives and readiness to cooperate with, caution, or oppose U.S. and ROK actions in a
severe crisis) constitutes one of the largest uncertainties faced by
Washington and Seoul.  The Chinese have reason to pursue loose
diplomatic coordination with the United States and ROK (witness,
for example, China's constructive role in the four-party talks), and
this might extend to consultations over humanitarian assistance in
the absence of major crisis.  But Chinese responses to internal
upheaval in the North that threatened to spill outward could prove
highly "scenario dependent."  For example, though the Chinese
would seem to have ample reason to avoid direct embroilment in
North Korean internal affairs, their incentives to control and contain
a potential humanitarian crisis near their border with the North
seem self-evident.  Increased refugee flows into China have led to
crackdowns by Chinese security personnel against some of these
refugees, some of whom are accused of various criminal activities.[20]
Moreover, in the absence of credible strategic understandings among
the United States, China, and the ROK on a range of concerns (e.g.,
control of WMD assets, possible deployment of U.S. and ROK forces
north of the 38th parallel, acute humanitarian concerns that could
prompt unilateral U.S. and ROK actions, and border control in contingencies short of war), it seems highly questionable that the Chinese would remain passive or immobilized.  Thus, regardless of how
China seeks to facilitate preferred outcomes in the absence of major
internal change in the North, these nearer-term policies are not a full

---

[20]See, for example, the comments of Wu Dawei, China's ambassador to the ROK, in a
South Korean television interview, January 30, 1999, in BBC *Selected World Broadcasts*,
No. 3449, February 3, 1999, pp. D1–D3. According to Ambassador Wu, "after coming
to China, some North Koreans are not returning home, which has become a problem.
We are taking measures regarding this matter. They are not refugees. Because they are
North Korean citizens, the assistance we can give them is very limited." Estimates of
the numbers of North Koreans illegally residing in northeastern China range as high as
100,000, with even larger numbers making regular forays into China in search of food.
For a graphic account, see Shim Jae Hoon, "A Crack in the Wall," *Far Eastern Economic
Review,* April 29, 1999, pp. 10–14.

or reliable predictor of future behavior if Beijing should conclude that its vital interests are at risk.[21]

Finally, there is the Russia factor. For much of the Cold War, Moscow was Pyongyang's largest benefactor. With the collapse of the Soviet Union, however, Moscow became progressively more marginalized in its peninsular role. Indeed, given the substantial (and growing) ROK economic interactions with China, Russia is no longer able to compete credibly with its neighbor for the attention of the South. Russia feels excluded from policy developments on the peninsula in a number of realms: the KEDO process has blocked possible Russian reactor sales to the North; Moscow (as well as Tokyo) has no seat at the four-party talks; and Russia's economic and security linkages with the North have clearly diminished. This said, Russia may well retain some historical linkages to senior North Korean officials, though these could prove a diminishing asset. But Russian pronouncements assert a continued strategic interest in relation to longer-term regional security and in the context of how the unification process might unfold.[22] The more immediate issue, however, is whether and how Russia could be credibly involved in future peninsular outcomes. Unlike the 1961 treaty of alliance and mutual assistance, the new treaty on interstate relations initialed in March 1999 commits Russia to consultations with the North in the event of a crisis, but it does not obligate Russia to automatic military involvement.[23] Thus, it is far from certain that major internal change in the North—especially if it produced larger external repercussions—would appreciably increase Russia's leverage and in-

---

[21]Most published Chinese assessments on Korea remain highly elliptical on these issues. For a notable exception, see Zhao Gancheng, "The Korea Unification and China's Options," *SIIS Journal,* Vol. 2, No. 2, July 1996, pp. 35–51. Most of the more candid Chinese commentaries on Korea are conveyed in private discussion. For a useful and revealing summary, see *Sino-American Cooperation on the Korean Peninsula: Prospects and Obstacles,* Asia-Pacific Center for Security Studies and United States Institute of Peace: Conference Report on U.S.-China Security Cooperation in Northeast Asia, Honolulu, Hawaii, May 26–28, 1998.

[22]For a useful assessment, see Vadim Tkachenko, "The Consequences of Korea's Unification for Russia and Security in Northeast Asia," *Far Eastern Affairs,* No. 4, 1997, pp. 23–40.

[23]For details on the new treaty, consult Itar-Tass, March 17, 1999, in BBC *Summary of World Broadcasts,* No. 3486, March 18, 1999, p. D2; see also the remarks of Russian Deputy Foreign Minister Grigoriy Karasin, Kyoto, April 2, 1999, in BBC *Summary of World Broadcasts,* No. 3500, April 5, 1999, p. E1.

volvement, given Moscow's own internal preoccupations.  But a surviving and recovering North could well see opportunities to strengthen its links to Russia, suggesting one means by which Moscow could reemerge as a more credible actor on the peninsula.

For all involved powers, the unease about Korean unification reflects the latent dangers and risks associated with this prospect.  The combination of factors seems especially volatile:  two political and economic systems that for a half century have been completely divided and highly antagonistic, notwithstanding their shared ethnic, linguistic, and family identities; a still unresolved military conflict, for which both sides have continued to plan and prepare for over the past 45 years; and prodigious military capabilities poised across a narrow armistice line (including extensive WMD holdings in the North) that could spur an extremely violent armed conflict.  These conditions give rise to understandable concern about the risks of a disorderly unification process.  Confronted with such potentially ominous circumstances, it seems no surprise that all involved powers publicly advocate a gradualist approach to unification, which would therefore appear to ensure the indefinite division of the peninsula.

This collective resort to the political and security equivalent of a default option might well be indefinitely sustainable were it not for the North's mounting internal vulnerabilities and the latent threat of instability they create.  In Korea we no longer witness a competition between two distinct political and economic systems capable of sustaining an open-ended rivalry.  The North is a failed regime that (given its deeply entrenched control apparatus and its still-intact military capabilities) has thus far been able to persevere.  Though an array of factors could yet shatter the veneer of stability over one of the world's most closed and secretive political systems, these events have yet to materialize.  The onset of such destabilizing change—with all the unpredictable following consequences—is thus among the central concerns of our analysis.

This study, however, makes no effort to predict the precise circumstances that could stimulate major change.  Our objectives are instead to (1) identify and characterize alternative scenarios for the peninsula that we believe are now credible possibilities; (2) specify some of the possible signposts or indicators that might suggest movement toward a given path or direction; (3) sketch out plausible sequences of change that could result under these circumstances; (4) assess how these shifting circumstances might alter the calculus of gain and risk among all relevant states; and (5) identify some of the more salient operational implications of different scenarios for U.S. and ROK defense planning, with particular attention to future U.S. Army requirements.

## IMPLICATIONS FOR U.S. AND ROK DEFENSE PLANNING

The analysis to this point has indirectly suggested some of the reasons favoring pursuit of an engagement strategy with the North. Preferred outcomes (for example, a significant reduction in the military threat, stabilization and reform in North Korea, major gains in South-North relations, and improved ties between North Korea and the United States) seem fairly self-evident. But movement toward an endgame in which all sides achieve an acceptable outcome at tolerable levels of political, military, and economic risk and commitment cannot obviate the need for planning against very divergent possibilities. Three challenges in particular warrant closer attention.

First, future defense planning has to assess how current deterrence and defense capabilities need to be reconfigured in response to unconventional scenarios or to major deviations within familiar scenarios. Capabilities-based planning must not be neglected, but given the range of military threats faced by the U.S.-ROK Combined Forces Command (CFC), an acceleration of internal change in North Korea or asymmetric threats could have strategic consequences that severely complicate or degrade current defense options. *Military capabilities matter, but their net utility will be tied heavily to actions undertaken by leaders in Pyongyang or triggered by internal developments in the North, and may have limited or marginal relevance to current planning scenarios under certain conditions.*

Second, linear projections of security futures on the peninsula, including postunification defense requirements, will have substantially less utility if the future unfolds in a more discontinuous way. We characterize this process as the "unification tunnel," with the tunnel metaphor describing a cumulative but rapidly accelerating transformation between the two Koreas that results ultimately in a unified peninsula. Thus, a triggering event or series of events could begin a chain reaction that expedites unification. But the tunnel image also illustrates how uncertainties and unknowns today could become certain and known under more constrained circumstances: we do not see entry into the tunnel permitting abrupt exit, especially as the larger process of change begins to unfold. The experiences in Eastern Europe and the former Soviet Union during the late 1980s and early 1990s are a possible guide in this respect. An incremental transformation remains very unlikely in North Korea, and a process of compressed change on the peninsula could result in abrupt unification. Even though all external actors clearly prefer a gradual reduction of tensions leading to integration and a political *modus vivendi*, the latent possibility of rapid unification remains, and it is increasing over time. Assuming that unification occurs quickly and with little warning, and that South Korea emerges as the successor state, all powers, including the United States, will need to quickly prepare for the postunification era. *Security planning throughout the "unification tunnel" process therefore has to allow for greater flexibility and adaptability than in any previous period.*

Third, the United States and South Korea will confront new alliance management requirements, including political and military responses if and when peninsular stability is seriously threatened. Systemic instability in North Korea would involve virtually every level of the two governments involved in alliance relations as well as the military forces of both countries. In addition, the concerns of various regional powers would increase substantially in a severe crisis, depending on the depth and speed of change in the North. This is particularly true for China, given its shared border and its long-standing historical ties with North Korea. If a crisis should escalate into a military clash or expand into a major conflict, Japan's role will also be critical in the context of a range of support requirements for U.S. forces. Despite Russia's limited political or military roles at present, Moscow also continues to maintain ties with the North and may feel compelled to react in order to secure its own interests in a major Korean crisis.

Thus, U.S.-South Korean joint planning and coordination may be insufficient to address a range of potential outcomes that are now much more plausible than in the past. The alliance must therefore be prepared to cope with rapid unification and a spectrum of new issues that will surface in the postunification era. A host of factors—

the size, composition, and location of U.S. forces in a unified Korea; future political and command arrangements; strategic and operational adjustments for U.S. forces in Korea and elsewhere in the region; managing rapid demobilization in the North; dismantling North Korea's WMD infrastructure; and many other pressing military and security issues—will have to be addressed between the United States and a unified Korea. *Managing the U.S.-ROK alliance will require a very different frame of reference for these issues.* To the maximum extent feasible, the two sides need to jointly conceptualize security planning dynamics for the postunification era now, before the process of internal change in the North gathers momentum.

The unification of Korea could also emerge as a pivotal geopolitical factor in the strategic equation of Northeast Asia in the early 21st century. If Korea is unified in the near future, it will be the first time in nearly one hundred years that it has been a single, independent actor, though the challenges of achieving a credible integration of the two systems are likely to prove prodigious and long term. In turn, adjustments are inevitable in major power strategies toward the peninsula and a unified Korea's strategic and economic ties with the United States, China, Japan, and Russia. Great-power competition focusing on Korea began to intensify in the 1880s, when denying rival powers control over the peninsula became a critical political and military objective among contending states. After defeating its two rivals (Czarist Russia and Qing China), Japan emerged as the predominant East Asian power and promptly colonized Korea in 1910. Liberation in 1945 quickly led to partition and, in 1950, to war. Since that time, virtually every dimension of Korean security has been shaped by the politics and dynamics of a divided Korea. Although some of the legacies of the division are likely to persist (in particular the alliance with the United States), a unified Korea may become more nationalistic and could pursue a more diversified national strategy. For example, owing to historical, strategic, and economic considerations, a unified Korea might pursue a closer relationship with China, even if it maintains a primary affiliation with the United States.

Unification would therefore pose unprecedented challenges to Korea. Compared to a foreign policy and security strategy that has been anchored firmly to the U.S.-Korean alliance for decades, prioritizing and implementing an overall strategy for a unified Korea is bound to become more complex. Strategic flexibility could be enhanced, but Korean policymakers might prove maladept at maneuvering among (let alone exploiting) major power rivalries. Moreover, Korea's postunification strategies could directly impinge upon the security interests of its more powerful neighbors. For instance, although North Korea's ballistic missile program has implications beyond the Korean peninsula, the two Koreas' military buildup has been arrayed almost exclusively against each other and not against China, Japan, or Russia. In the postunification era, Korea's force modernization and power projection capabilities will come under much closer scrutiny by its neighbors. Though it may be premature for Korea to articulate its strategic priorities under conditions of unification, it is not too soon for the United States and ROK to begin assessing such possibilities for their respective interests and to weigh how the outcome of the half-century of confrontation between South and North will shape the longer term.

## SOUTH KOREA'S ECONOMIC CRISIS AND ITS SECURITY RAMIFICATIONS

The uncertainties on the Korean peninsula have been compounded by the East Asian financial and economic crisis. As the world's 11th largest economy, South Korea was the most industrialized of East Asia's "Four Tigers," and it had continued to register GDP growth rates averaging 6 to 7 percent throughout the early and middle 1990s. Notwithstanding Korea's highly credible macroeconomic performance, a surge in short-term international debt, estimated by the International Monetary Fund (IMF) at $157 billion, triggered a major crisis.[24]  South Korea's backward financial and banking systems, political corruption, bankruptcies among several leading *chaebols* (conglomerates), and rising wages (the second highest in East Asia after Japan) all contributed to a rapid deterioration in economic conditions during the fall of 1997.

Indeed, many telling indications of the looming crisis were evident months before the onset of the larger East Asian crisis triggered by the collapse of the Thai currency in July 1997. The bankruptcy of the

---

[24]Some analysts assert that the actual figure is probably higher, given that it does not take into account debts held by offshore Korean companies.

Hanbo Group in January 1997, as described by one well-informed economic observer, "revealed many weaknesses of the Korean economic system to the international financial community, such as excessive reliance on bank borrowing by conglomerates, political collusion between conglomerates and politicians, lack of transparency in business accounts, and ineffective bank supervisory mechanisms."[25] The critical issues over the longer run are twofold: first, the rate of recovery in the economy as a whole (unemployment is approaching 2 million workers, its highest level in over three decades, with the economy contracting by 5.8 percent during 1998[26]), and the capability of the ROK's political leadership to address the deeper maladies affecting the business climate. Despite unexpectedly robust economic growth during early 1999, fueled by strong export performance and major increases in foreign direct investment, the longer-term economic challenges remain substantial.

The economic crisis also entailed substantial national security implications. The government has deferred a number of force modernization programs, and additional cutbacks are likely for at least the next two years. The ROK Ministry of National Defense has also announced cuts in the planned acquisition of AWACS early-warning aircraft for the air force and next-generation submarines for the navy.[27] Indeed, the defense ministry's budget plan for 1999 shows a 0.4 percent decrease in defense spending, the first decrease ever recorded in the ROK's fifty-year history. Though Korean defense planners project renewed budgetary growth in the five-year plan that begins in the year 2000, these outcomes will remain contingent on future economic performance.[28] Thus, if South Korea's economic

---

[25]Sung-Mok Suh, *The Korean Economic Crisis: What Can We Learn From It?* (Stanford: Asia/Pacific Research Center, Stanford University, May 1998), p. 12. Suh's reconstruction of the crisis and its consequences is first-rate.

[26]Michael Schuman, "South Korea's Economy May Have Turned a Corner," *The Asian Wall Street Journal*, March 24, 1999.

[27]*Chosun Ilbo*, January 12, 1998.

[28]"Defense Ministry Proposes First-Ever Budget Cuts," *The Korea Herald*, September 22, 1998. The annual increases in defense expenditure in the past had ranged between 9.3 percent to 12.6 percent. The growth in 1998 was 0.1 percent. The budget for the year 2000 projects an increase of 5.5 percent with an average annual increase over the full five-year defense plan between 4 and 5 percent. Yonhap, February 12, 1999, in BBC *Summary of World Broadcasts*, No. 3458, February 13, 1999, p. D4.

recovery proceeds more slowly than is currently anticipated, there could be longer-term security repercussions.

For example, if a major political or military crisis erupts in North Korea within the next two or three years, it could severely strain South Korea's crisis-management capabilities and responses. In contrast to most of the rapidly developing East Asian economies, South Korea has sought to maintain a diversified industrial base and is a major player in such areas as steel, ship building, automobiles, consumer electronics, petrochemicals, heavy machinery, and construction. But the South Korean economy's greatest vulnerabilities are in the financial sector, especially its highly sheltered banking industry and the close relationships among the government, the conglomerates, and banks. These interconnections could therefore have a cascading effect on the economy as a whole, especially under much more stressful conditions or outright crisis in the North.

The ROK's current economic preoccupations have reinforced widespread unease about "unification through absorption." Even before the outbreak of the economic crisis, there was a growing internal consensus that unification costs could prove prohibitive for South Korea. In the aftermath of the crisis and the significant financial burden posed by South Korea's need to pay back loans to the IMF and other agencies, it remains doubtful that South Korea could afford to absorb the North solely on the basis of its own resources. In this respect, President Kim's policy initiatives toward the North have made a virtue out of necessity. Thus, the strategy of engagement, including support for a "soft landing" in the North, could gain additional political momentum in the United States and South Korea, even as it rests on highly problematic assumptions.[29]

The full impact of the economic crisis on longer-term defense modernization goals for South Korea is still difficult to determine, given that most ongoing force upgrade programs were decided before the crisis. For at least the next two to three fiscal years, however, defense budget cuts will be sustained in most East Asian countries. For South Korea, some elements of long-term force planning (including some postunification objectives) will need to be reconfigured. Even in the

---

[29]The concept of "soft landing" is discussed at greater length in Chapter Two.

nearer term, constraints on some defense acquisitions could inhibit South Korea's military response options in an acute peninsular crisis.

South Korea's economic setbacks also have ramifications for the U.S.-ROK alliance. On the one hand, the level of defense cooperation is unlikely to change and could even be enhanced, given uncertainties in North Korea. But if major economic difficulties persist, popular resentment against the major powers, especially the United States, could increase. Given popular perceptions of South Korea's already heavy dependence on the United States in defense and trade issues—some 56 percent responded in an opinion poll that South Korea's biggest foreign policy issue was the "high level of dependence on the United States"—public opinion could trigger resentment toward the United States and the U.S.-ROK alliance.[30] President Kim has sought to dampen these tendencies, but his ability to deflect them will ultimately rest on South Korea's economic performance, not declaratory policy pronouncements.

Notwithstanding the economic, political, and security dimensions of South Korea's current economic adjustment, the prospect of major change on the peninsula and even of unification will have a dynamic all its own. The purpose of this study is not to forecast the timing of major change or to predict a particular scenario or course of action. Rather, the principal objective is to highlight how key processes of change on the Korean peninsula and salient characteristics of different outcomes could trigger an array of consequences, including many that would severely test long-standing plans and policies. This study therefore has four main components, as outlined below.

- It examines four basic scenarios on the Korean peninsula that could lead to unification:

  — peaceful integration and unification;

  — collapse and unification through absorption;

  — unification through conflict;

  — disequilibrium with potential external intervention.

---

[30]This finding emerged from public opinion polling conducted in South Korea as part of a RAND Center for Asia-Pacific Policy research project.

- It assesses U.S.-ROK relations in each of the four scenarios while also evaluating China's potential responses to each.

- It identifies the strategic and operational implications for the U.S. Army, including appropriate military responses.

- It examines postunification dynamics, including how unification could affect the continued deployment of U.S. forces in Korea, the strategic and operational challenges that the Army could face after unification, and the characteristics of U.S.-ROK military cooperation after unification.

# Chapter Two

# THE NORTH KOREAN CONUNDRUM

## PYONGYANG'S DEEPENING CRISIS

North Korea is a juxtaposition of stark contradictions. Although the country has the world's fourth-largest military establishment with more than 1.1 million soldiers, an array of WMD capabilities (including a potential nuclear capability), and a population that is on near-constant war alert, the North Korean economy is experiencing acute atrophy and decline, including massive shortages in food production and a virtually moribund industrial structure. In the aftermath of the Cold War, North Korea confronted a major deterioration in its strategic environment. Moscow and Beijing were no longer prepared to compete for political ascendancy in Pyongyang, and both sharply curtailed their previous economic subsidies to the North. North Korea's erstwhile allies also vigorously cultivated ties with the South, culminating in the ROK's diplomatic recognition by both states.

At the same time, Pyongyang grimly upheld its self-reliance policies, to the ever-increasing detriment of its people; it moved to enshrine the dynastic succession from father to son; and it steadily amassed a WMD potential while also exporting ballistic missiles to South Asia, the Persian Gulf, and the Middle East. Despite its growing isolation and its problematic conduct at home and abroad, the North was able to negotiate skillfully and resourcefully with the United States during 1993–1994, turning a threat to withdraw from the Nuclear Non-Proliferation Treaty into a diplomatic opening with Washington, including energy and economic commitments. All such activities were undertaken with (at best) perfunctory, tactical adjustments in relations with the South, and with no evident change in its military strategy directed against the ROK.

Were it not for North Korea's military power, its capability to launch a highly destructive war against the ROK, and the strategic location of the Korean peninsula, the country would warrant only limited attention from the outside world. But Pyongyang's internal dynamics— and, even more fundamentally, its capability to persevere—are increasingly the focal point of international attention, and the potential fulcrum of longer-term change on the peninsula. How North Korea copes (or fails to cope) with its daunting political and economic challenges in the coming few years will likely prove pivotal to the stability and security of the peninsula. The regime's decisions and actions will also shape the resultant security priorities of the U.S.- ROK alliance.

Kim Jong Il stands at the epicenter of this process.[1] Few political systems are as dependent on the whims, perceptions, and decisions of a single leader. To be sure, systemic conditions (in particular, North Korea's worsening economic plight and the potential for a political challenge to Kim's authority in the event of further decline) must also be considered. But virtually no dimension of North Korea's present policies or future prospects can be assessed without direct reference to Kim Jong Il. How North Korea addresses its economic problems; its willingness to deal with the government in Seoul; its force modernization goals and programs; and its principal foreign policy objectives cannot be understood apart from Kim Jong Il and the political and security apparatus on which he relies.

The extreme personalization of power in Pyongyang therefore emerges as a crucial factor in assessing North Korea's goals and policy options—to the extent that a system intent on survival is capable of defining and implementing coherent national policies. In a fundamental sense, North Korea confronts four main dilemmas:

---

[1]For vivid testimony on the centrality of Kim Jong Il's role, see the interview with Hwang Jang-yup, former secretary of the Korean Workers' Party, conducted by the Japanese journalist Ryo Hagiwara on December 10, 1998, and published in *Bungei Shunju*, February 1999, pp. 324–346. The interview is translated in the Foreign Broadcast Information Service *Daily Report*, FBIS-EAS-1999-0210.

- Sustaining an increasingly sclerotic command economy while continuing to invest nearly 25 percent of a dwindling GNP on defense.

- Attempting to compensate for acute structural problems in the economy (including a dysfunctional production and distribution system) without inducing a loss of central political control that could threaten the regime's hold on power.

- Continuing to participate in bilateral and multilateral accords and negotiations (e.g., the October 1994 Agreed Framework, the Korean Peninsula Energy Development Organization, and the four-party talks), thereby gaining additional international assistance, while avoiding concessions that would undermine Pyongyang's larger diplomatic and military strategies.

- Maintaining its foreign policy opening to the United States while avoiding full-scale relations with South Korea that could undermine the North's national sovereignty and exclusive claims to legitimacy on the peninsula.

Since the death in July 1994 of Kim Il Sung, the founder and "Great Leader" of North Korea for nearly fifty years, North Korean politics, economics, and strategy have received a major upsurge in attention. Even acknowledging the very limited and problematic quality of the available data, North Korea defies easy characterization. As a leading U.S. expert on East Asia has observed, "[I]n our post-revolutionary era a few states remain outside the mainstream, zealously guarding their past even as they are forced to adapt selectively to the present. None fit that category more fully than North Korea."[2] Thus, despite widespread expectations that Kim Jong Il would face political challenges to his ascendancy or that he would have to make major concessions to the outside world to garner international assistance, the North Korean regime continues to function largely according to its own norms, procedures, expectations, and timetable.

Kim Jong Il assumed the post of General Secretary of the Korean Workers' Party (KWP) in October 1997, formalizing his leadership of the party. While this event signaled the culmination of the first suc-

---

[2]Robert A. Scalapino, *North Korea at a Crossroads* (Stanford, CA: Hoover Institution Press, 1997), p. 1.

cessful dynastic succession in the communist world and the official beginning of the Kim Jong Il era, it also symbolized the official end of the Kim Il Sung era.[3] Kim Jong Il's status was further enhanced at the meeting of the Supreme People's Assembly (SPA) in September 1998, when he inherited the mantle of state authority, though the title of "president" was left in perpetuity for the deceased Kim Il Sung. Kim Jong Il also installed in power an array of senior officials for positions that had been vacant for some time, including the premier and the defense minister.[4] Thus, North Korea's future, and quite possibly the fate of the system itself, will remain inextricably tied to the actions and political fortunes of Kim Jong Il and his closest subordinates.

Major changes in the international system, including the dissolution of the Soviet Union and China's rapid economic and political development, have also profoundly redefined the North's political and strategic options in the 1990s. Pyongyang's decades-long reliance on subsidized trade with its two major patrons plummeted rapidly after the former Soviet Union and China began to demand hard currency payments in 1991–1992 for exports such as oil and grain, without the North having an alternative source of financial support.[5] As China enunciated a more pragmatic posture toward South Korea and developed an increasingly robust economic relationship there, North Korea made some grudging diplomatic adjustments, such as consenting to join the United Nations in 1990 simultaneous with Seoul's admission and signing a series of confidence-building measures with the South in 1991. The outbreak of the North Korean nuclear crisis in March 1993, when Pyongyang initially threatened to withdraw from

---

[3]Although nepotism was especially prevalent in two East European governments prior to 1989 (Romania and Albania), neither achieved a dynastic succession. Before his family's ouster and his own execution in 1989, Nicolae Ceausescu groomed his son to eventually succeed him, while his wife remained the second in command. Albania's Hoxha regime ended with his wife's detention in 1990. Fidel Castro's brother, minister of defense Raul Castro, has been groomed as his successor, although it remains to be seen how Cuba will be transformed after Castro's death. But North Korea stands out as the only communist country so far to achieve a successful dynastic transfer of power.

[4]For a useful summary, see the DPRK Report prepared by the Center for Contemporary International Problems of the Russian Diplomatic Academy, No. 14, September–October 1998, subsequently published as a *NAPS Network Special Report*, October 20, 1998.

[5]See, in particular, Noland, Robinson, and Wang, *Rigorous Speculation.*

the Nuclear Non-Proliferation Treaty (NPT), and the prolonged negotiations involving the two Koreas and the United States, galvanized the interest of the intelligence, policymaking, and research communities in North Korean politics, foreign affairs, and security policies.

By mid-decade, accelerated economic decline, severe shortages of energy and food, and the death of Kim Il Sung had heightened attention to the possibility of a North Korean collapse (also referred to as the "hard landing" scenario). Many analysts seemed convinced that North Korea was on borrowed time. There was much analysis of the conditions under which North Korea might collapse and the potential effects of an implosion, including the costs that would be associated with the South's absorbing the North in a manner akin to German unification. Domestic political change in South Korea, beginning with a peaceful transfer of power in 1988 and followed by gradual democratization, had also slowly opened up the terms of domestic debate on North Korea. Hitherto limited access to North Korean source materials was steadily eased, enabling a more diverse range of analysis and reporting in ROK academic and media circles. This trend has accelerated throughout the 1990s, permitting a much fuller set of judgments and observations to enter the policy debate.

## THE STRATEGIC CONSEQUENCES OF NORTH KOREA'S ECONOMIC DECLINE

Three basic questions have preoccupied North Korea watchers during the early and middle 1990s:

- Does North Korea have the capacity to undertake meaningful economic reform (i.e., the creation of special economic zones, less rigid adherence to collectivization, and increased receptivity to foreign economic involvement) without undermining the legitimacy of the Kim Jong Il regime and hence political stability?

- Despite North Korea's continued adherence to the *juche* (self-reliance) ideology in defense and foreign policy, how much flexibility and accommodation is Pyongyang prepared to show in its political and diplomatic actions, especially with the United States?

- Given North Korea's deeply rooted economic problems and resistance to more wide-ranging change, will the capabilities of the
  party, state, and army remain resilient enough to withstand and
  overcome the economic deprivation currently engulfing society
  as a whole?

Among these questions, the first may ultimately prove the most important, since it is likely to have the largest long-term effect on the
fate of the North Korean system.  In essence, can North Korea (in
conjunction with increased international aid flows) muddle through
its continued economic decline, or is the status quo fundamentally
unsustainable?

The economic issue entails two fundamental questions:  the *desirability* of economic reforms and the *capacity* to undertake reforms.
Numerous analysts have drawn attention to measures such as the
Rajin-Sonbong special economic zone plan, joint ventures with foreign companies, growing inter-Korean trade, and limited signs of
privatization in the agricultural sector.  Others have focused on
North Korea's ability to move toward a more hybrid economic system and more flexible political arrangements.  With the increased
flexibility of ROK policy toward the North, several South Korean
*chaebols* (most notably, the Hyundai Group) have initiated economic
collaboration in the North that, if fully consummated, will entail
major infusions of hard-currency resources into various projects in
the North.[6]  North Korea's overall strategy toward South Korea has
undergone repeated redefinition over the past half century: a "use of
force phase" (1945–1953), "peace offensive phase" (1954–1961),
"revolutionary strategy phase" (1962–1969), "negotiation phase,"
(1970–1979), "confederation phase" (1980–1989), and "coexistence
phase" (1988 to the present).[7]  The question is whether the North's
steady economic decline throughout the 1990s will compel yet another redefinition of policy toward the South.  Some analysts, for example, attach significance to North Korea's 1991 decision to jointly
enter the United Nations with South Korea and to increases in South-

---

[6]See "True Beginning," *Korea Newsreview,* November 7, 1998, pp. 8–9.

[7]Moon-Young Hun, "Bukhan eui Byunhwa-wa Daenam Jeongchek Jeonmang,"
["Prospects for Change in North Korea and Its Policy Towards the South"], *Jeolryak
Yeonku* [Strategic Studies], Vol. 3, No. 2, Spring 1996, p. 114.

North trade from just over $1 million in 1988 to $114 million in 1996 to $300 million in 1997.[8]  Others see an emergent pattern of policy actions including the December 1991 Basic Accord, the most wide-ranging confidence-building agreement between the South and North; the October 1994 Agreed Framework between the United States and North Korea, which was able to freeze North Korea's near-term plutonium production for its nuclear weapons program; and Pyongyang's participation in the four-party talks.

There is still no consensus among analysts on the degree of policy change North Korea can undertake without affecting political stability.  However, the steady contraction of the North Korean economy throughout the 1990s is beyond dispute: 1990 (–3.7%), 1991 (–5.1%), 1992 (–7.7%), 1993 (–4.2%), 1994 (–1.8%), 1995 (–4.6%), 1996 (–3.7%), 1997 (–6.8%).[9]  While debate continues on the origins and magnitude of North Korea's food crisis and how the international community can best provide help, the persistence of acute grain shortages during the 1990s is incontestable.  But the consequences of these shortages (in terms of the extent of deprivation and starvation) have been subject to hugely discrepant judgments among relief agencies and nongovernmental organizations overseeing food assistance programs to the North, with estimates ranging from tens of thousands to more than two million who have purportedly died from starvation. Acute energy shortages have also become a virtual constant.  For example, the excavation of coal—the major source of household and commercial heating in the North—dropped from a high of 37.5 million tons in 1984 to 25.4 million tons in 1994.  In turn, virtually all dimensions of the North Korean industrial economy have been affected, including a sharp loss of electrical power, a 30 percent plant

---

[8]*Nambuk Han Kyungje Saehoeang Bikyo* [A Comparison of South and North Korea's Economic and Social Indicators] (Seoul: Bureau of Statistics, November 1996), p. 108; "Economic Cooperation Between Two Koreas," *Korean Unification Bulletin,* September 1998, p. 3.  However, South Korea's economic downturn sharply reduced this commerce in the first half of 1998, especially ROK imports of metal ore and agricultural products from the North.

[9]Data on the North Korean economy continue to be debated by analysts, although all agree that the economy has been shrinking since the early 1990s.  North Korea's negative GNP figures since 1990 were compiled from *Nambuk Han Kyungje Saehoeang Bikyo* [A Comparison of South and North Korea's Economic and Social Indicators] (Seoul: Bureau of Statistics, November 1996) and sources from the Ministry of Unification.  See also *The Asian Wall Street Journal,* May 28–29, 1999, p. 5.

operation rate, substantially decreased steel production, and a steep decline in oil imports.[10]

There seems to be an emerging consensus that deteriorating economic conditions are a necessary but not sufficient condition for a collapse.  Since the early 1990s, various reasons have been put forward to account for the resilience of the North Korean system:  a very efficient control and surveillance apparatus; economic support from China; decreasing but still significant capital inflows from pro–North Korean residents in Japan; and international food aid and energy assistance have all been cited.  North Korea's unique brand of socialism appears to be without historical precedent, particularly as it pertains to sustaining a near-total war footing on an open-ended basis.  The extremely high degree of social and political control has been a major factor enabling North Korea to persist through its prolonged economic decline.  Although North Korea has thus far managed to keep political or social disruptions to a minimum, an economy and polity under such severe strain may ultimately succumb to the pressure.[11]

## IMPEDIMENTS AND RISKS TO A REFORM STRATEGY

To cope with these extraordinary challenges, North Korea has adopted what one observer has described as a strategy of "system-defending reform."  This survival strategy has attempted to preserve the core characteristics of the DPRK:  maintaining the command economy; continuing to allocate disproportionate resources to the defense sector; relying heavily on ideological incentives and harsh police control over the work force; and continuing modest levels of trade with the ROK while severely limiting major ROK investment.[12] The question is whether these measures can be sustained indefi-

---

[10]Soo-Young Choi, "Bukhan eui Sahoe-Kyungje Kuhowa Hyunhwang" [The Current Status of North Korea's Social and Economic Infrastructure], *Jeolryak Yeonku* [Strategic Studies], Vol. 3, No. 2, Spring 1996, p. 47.

[11]For further discussion, see Nicholas Eberstadt, "The DPRK as an Economy Under Multiple Severe Stresses:  Analogies and Lessons from Past and Recent Historical Experience," *The Korean Journal of National Unification,* Vol. 6, October 1997, pp. 87–89.

[12]Adrian Buzo, "Economic Reform in the DPRK," *The Economics of Korean Unification,* Vol. 2, No. 1, Spring 1997, p. 63.

nitely, whether leaders will ultimately be compelled to make a larger set of adaptations, or whether internal stresses and pressures might simply overwhelm the system as a whole.

Over the short to medium term, North Korea has three broad policy options: (1) initiate widespread economic reforms; (2) maintain the status quo with only marginal change in order to overcome severe food shortages and related difficulties; or (3) follow a hybrid alternative that enables it to muddle through the worst of the current economic crisis, including greatly increased reliance on international assistance.[13] While a more flexible, market-oriented strategy would seem likely to generate the largest results, it also would entail the highest political risks. By contrast, either the muddling-through or the hybrid alternative could provide some relief through: increased international assistance (especially from China); the creation of a few free-trade zones, thereby earning much-needed hard currency; and selective engagement with South Korea, especially in tourism and enhanced involvment by South Korean industrial conglomerates in development projects in the North. Finally, North Korea could opt simply to defend the status quo. Such a decision, however, would likely exacerbate an already serious situation, since economic decay would only become more acute.

Given the prohibitive political costs of undertaking wide-ranging reforms and the potential implications for regime survival, the Kim Jong Il regime is highly unlikely to pursue reforms akin to those pursued by China. It is important to recall that China's "four modernizations" strategy began only after the death of Mao Zedong. But because Kim Jong Il's political legitimacy cannot be separated from the legacy of Kim Il Sung, instituting economic policies that run against virtually every tenet of *juche* would be tantamount to destroying the political essence of the Kim Jong Il regime. Indeed, whereas China and the former Soviet Union both underwent major changes in political leadership, North Korea continues to be ruled by the Kim dy-

---

[13]Various scholars have offered estimates about the future of North Korea, ranging from imminent collapse to prolonged uncertainty, some type of collapse or implosion, or even conflict in the aftermath of a collapse. For one of the more provocative treatments of North Korea's ability to survive, see Marcus Noland, "Why North Korea Will Muddle Through," *Foreign Affairs*, Vol. 76, No. 4, July/August 1997, especially pp. 110–116.

nasty.  For example, in June 1997, just before the third anniversary of Kim Il Sung's death, the North Korean media repeatedly stressed that despite the Great Leader's death, "our people have the high pride of being eternal family members of the Great Leader Comrade Kim Il-song in the past and present" and, further, that "our people are a people who know only of the lineage of the great leader and of *juche*, and who succeed that lineage."[14]  Indeed, in a speech given to Kim Il Sung University students in December 1996 on the occasion of the 50th anniversary of the school's founding, Kim Jong Il held "lethargic party functionaries and secretaries" responsible for North Korea's economic difficulties and exonerated himself of any responsibility:

> At this time, when the situation is complicated, I cannot solve all knotty problems while handling practical economic work.  I should take charge of the party, the Army, and other major sectors.  If I handle even practical economic work, it would have irreparable consequences on the revolution and construction.  *When he was alive, the leader* [suryongnim] *told me not to get involved in economic work.  He repeatedly told me that if I got involved in economic work, I would not be able to handle party and Army work properly.*  Strengthening the Army is more important than anything else given today's complicated situation.[15]

But Kim Jong Il did not offer any blueprint for remedying North Korea's acute economic woes, opting instead to stress that more revolutionary zeal at all levels of the party and emulation of the army's "undying and absolute sacrificing spirit" would lead to a "solution of current complications."  Thus, even if Kim Jong Il wanted to launch major changes, "a variety of considerations suggest that North Korea is unlikely to undertake wide-ranging reforms of its own volition."[16]  Russian and Chinese observers of North Korean affairs have echoed comparable doubts about the Kim Jong Il regime's ability to implement major economic reforms, although these specialists tend to

---

[14]"Our People Are Family Members of the Great Leader Forever," *Nodong Sinmun* [Workers' Daily], June 17, 1997, in FBIS-EAS-97-122, June 17, 1997, p. 3.

[15]"Text of Speech by Kim Chong-il, Delivered in December 1996 on Occasion of the 50th Anniversary of the Founding of Kim Il-song University," *Wolgan Chosun* [Monthly Chosun], April 1997, in FBIS-EAS-97-054, April 1, 1997, p. 6.  Emphasis added.

[16]Noland, "Why North Korea Will Muddle Through," p. 111.

place greater emphasis on North Korea's ability to survive. According to one former senior Russian diplomat, the issue is not whether North Korea is going to enact economic reforms along the lines of China, former East European countries, or even Russia. Rather, the regime has been able to ensure its survival by maintaining extremely tight social and political control, reinforcing ideological zeal in a hostile environment, accruing economic and political benefits from brinksmanship, and supporting a vast military.[17]

Whether North Korea will ultimately collapse, muddle through, reform successfully, or maintain the status quo for at least a decade is impossible to judge definitively. Perhaps an even more fundamental question is whether systemic decay has reached a point where undertaking marginal reforms or maintaining the present course of action will make little difference. As suggested previously, an objective measurement of North Korea's structural integrity or a precise forecast of the date of potential collapse is next to impossible, until overt manifestations of such collapse are fully evident. But a reasonably satisfactory estimate of systemic capabilities can be based on an analysis of five major issues:

- Kim Jong Il's leadership abilities, including major policy decisions since the death of Kim Il Sung as well as attitudes on liberalization and reform.

- The effectiveness of state control mechanisms, including enhanced surveillance, tight restrictions on population movement, controlling the number of defectors and refugees to the South and to China, and crushing any internal opposition.

- The role and place of ideology in North Korean society, including the internal functions of *juche* under Kim Jong Il and elite perceptions of his rule.

- The role of the *nomenklatura,* including potential political rivalries within the party, the army, and the bureaucracy, and the morale of the armed forces.

---

[17]See Vladimir P. Lukin, "On Scenarios of North Korea's Change," *North Korea: How Much Longer Can They Sustain?* (Seoul: Seoul Sinmun, 1997), pp. 162–163.

• The overall state of the North Korean economy, including the viability of the ration system, current and projected assistance from abroad (especially China), and reallocation of human capital and energy resources.[18]

Based on the above factors and assuming that the system's decline is not arrested, North Korea could ultimately confront a descending strategic spiral (see Figure 1) with six distinct stages:

1. Atrophy (in economic policymaking).

2. Economic breakdown (i.e., inability of the central government to maintain effective control).

3. Political instability (de facto challenge to or ouster of the Kim Jong Il regime).

4. Regime breakdown (failure of central government or party control and dissolution of party control over the armed forces).

5. Regime and/or state collapse (dissolution of the communist government, party, and armed forces).

6. Conflict or absorption.

Stages 1 through 3 constitute hallmarks of gradual strategic decay, whereas stages 4 through 6 represent manifestations of accelerated strategic decay.  North Korea today is between stages 1 and 2; that is, characteristics of atrophy and economic breakdown are fairly evident, but the society has yet to enter the critical stage of political instability.  But such a progression of events through the various stages does not have to occur sequentially: hence our use of "stages" rather than "phases," since the latter implies a specific temporal dimension and pattern to future events.  For example, political instability could emerge quite suddenly if threats to Kim Jong Il's rule appear in the form of an attempted coup.  Alternatively, widespread purges to ensure loyalty in the party and the army could instigate intrafamily disputes that in turn could feed into anti-Kim moves within the party,

_____

[18]See Song Young-Dae, "Sustainability of North Korea:  A Critical Analysis," *North Korea: How Much Longer Can They Sustain?* (Seoul:  Seoul Sinmun, September 1997), pp. 94–105.  Song served as the vice minister of unification from 1993 until 1996 in the Kim Young Sam government.

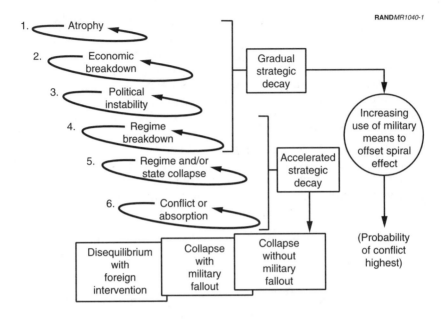

**Figure 1—North Korea's Descending Spiral**

the army, and the intelligence agencies. However, once political instability becomes widespread, regime collapse or even a state collapse could be accelerated. A major trigger event would set forces in motion that are likely to result in compressed developments (i.e., fast-paced events, with each stage quite short), with any number of permutations and potential outcomes.

## THE SOFT AND HARD LANDING DEBATE

Once the possibility of a North Korean collapse began to be discussed in earnest following the unification of Germany and the worsening economic conditions in the DPRK, a debate arose between advocates of the "hard landing" and "soft landing" schools. This debate has been stylized and is somewhat contrived. It has spawned a mini-lexicon of terms, for which there are few agreed-upon definitions, including "soft landing," "hard landing," "harder soft landing," "softer hard landing," and "no landing." Those who argue for the inevitability of a hard landing have stressed the highly centralized nature of the North Korean economic and political system, with its corresponding vulnerabilities stemming from decades of economic mismanagement and policy rigidity.  Proponents argue that because North Korea did not have the capacity to implement economic reforms without severe political or social repercussions, a collapse was virtually inevitable.  Conversely, those who foresee the possibility of a soft landing in the North emphasize that a collapse would be detrimental to all of the parties, including the two Koreas, the United States, China, Russia, and Japan.  Those who envisioned a soft-landing scenario argued that an appropriate mix of incentives combined with firm diplomacy and security policies could induce North Korea to enact economic reforms that would eventually allow its integration with other East Asian economies.

For analytic clarity, however, we need to attempt somewhat greater precision in terminology.  For the purposes of this study, the following definitions are used:

- **Hard landing.**  The inability of the regime in power to maintain effective political, economic, social, and military control, ultimately leading to the dissolution of the regime and, in the extreme case, the state.  Three variations could be posited:

  — A hard landing that results in a regime collapse, although the successor regime manages to retain political and military control.

  — A hard landing where political instability is rampant and where the successor regime is unable to retain effective control, so that there is no effective, central governing authority led either by the party, the bureaucracy, or the military.

  — A hard landing that could precipitate internal violence in the North or military operations against the South, up to and including large-scale war launched in desperation.

- **Soft landing.**  A process whereby gradual and controlled implementation of selective economic reforms enables a command economy to assume some characteristics of a market economy, although no regime change occurs.  Three variations seem possible:

— A soft landing that permits regime stabilization, without any descent into chaos or violence, either within or across the North's borders.

— A soft landing that transforms into a hard landing because the regime is ultimately unable to cope with mounting social, economic, and political demands arising from partial reforms.

— A soft landing that results in a weakened system with greater fragmentation (and regionalization) of the government and the party without leading to regime change.

• **No landing.** The maintenance of the status quo, where the regime is able to muddle through without enacting any major economic reforms, and with no major concessions in relations with the ROK. Such a scenario most likely correlates with the provision of sustained, substantial international aid to the North. The status quo is maintained indefinitely and the regime continues to remain in power. Two variations could be considered:

— Just as a soft landing could lead to a hard landing, a no landing could be transformed into a hard landing and a collapse.

— Maintaining the status quo for an extended time, however, is likely to result in further systemic decay, including an erosion of administrative and economic controls.

These alternative characterizations of potential outcomes on the Korean peninsula highlight the critical interconnections between regime stability and the security of the South. Indeed, the *leitmotif* of numerous policy initiatives toward the North throughout the 1990s has been to identify means to either diminish or defer the risks of acute instability, since the near-term preservation of peace (principally through preventive diplomacy) would leave open the possibility of subsequent transitions that would reduce the North Korean threat and avoid larger risks of war. Thus, the logic of engagement and the pursuit of a soft-landing strategy are closely connected. Four particular assumptions define this logic, as outlined below.

**Assumption 1:  Since the United States and South Korea share a common objective in avoiding war and fostering peaceful change on the Korean peninsula, an engagement strategy toward the North is the most appropriate policy option.** For example, as a joint U.S.-Korean study assessing the Agreed Framework stated:  "Despite its shortcomings and its uncertain future, it provides a mechanism for avoiding a nuclear weapons program in the North . . . and for the first time, a structure exists for a productive U.S.-DPRK relationship that could lead to a lessening of tension on the peninsula and promote better relations between North and South."[19]

**Assumption 2:  A soft landing, while far from assured, is not impossible, provided that the outside world offers adequate assurances and incentives to the North.  Moreover, given a choice between collapse or a soft landing, leaders in Pyongyang will ultimately opt for a soft landing.** An important corollary in this context is that the threat of war is driven primarily by North Korean anxieties about regime instability, accelerating economic difficulties, the absence of reliable allies, and South Korean dominance in the South-North competition.  As such, a combination of political, economic, and security inducements will ultimately enable North Korea to enact economic reforms, discard its rejectionist policies, and diminish its military threat against the South.

**Assumption 3:  North Korea's weapons development activities (in particular, its nuclear and missile programs) are designed more as bargaining chips to elicit increased economic assistance, rather than instruments of coercion or measures designed to ensure regime survival.** Any use of nuclear weapons by the North would be suicidal, since it would trigger large-scale retaliation by the United States.  The question, therefore, is whether the North Korean leadership believes its WMD capabilities confer significant political and military advantage, given that they could also largely constrain U.S. and ROK military options in a crisis.  But the corollary also applies:  a robust deterrence posture across a full spectrum of potential military actions will inhibit the North from launching an attack.

---

[19]Kyung Won Kim and Nicholas Platt, *Success or Sellout?  The U.S.–North Korean Nuclear Accord* (Seoul: Seoul Forum for International Affairs, 1995), p. 8.

**Assumption 4: Even if a soft landing does not materialize in North Korea, engagement with the North will prove crucial to minimizing the potential consequences of instability.** State collapse assumes widespread disintegration of the armed forces and (potentially) the South's inability to control residual military and paramilitary capabilities in various regions of the North. The success of efforts to avert major violence would depend on credible linkages to alternative sources of authority in the North. Though the dislocation and risks of internal violence should not be minimized in this scenario, linkages to domestic elites would enhance the possibility of less acute instability.

Despite the intrinsic appeal of the above strategy, it rests on assumptions and expectations that seem hugely optimistic. Although many observers believe that North Korea (notwithstanding its *juche* ideology) must ultimately reform to prevent further decay and systemic collapse, there is no automatic link between the need to undertake reform and the ability of the current regime to initiate reforms without suffering acute, and possibly fatal, damage to its political dominance. The crucial issue is not whether North Korea needs to revive its dysfunctional economy, but whether its current leadership can undertake meaningful reforms without endangering regime survival. As Kyung-Won Kim has emphasized, North Korea is unlikely to adopt a reform strategy for three basic reasons: (1) even if North Korea moved toward a market economy, there is no assurance that this would lead to improved economic performance; (2) even if reform should lead to better economic results, there is certain to be a considerable time lag before the full benefits would be achieved; and (3) substituting the strategy of opening and reform for the failed *juche* ideology would undermine North Korea's *raison d'être*. As Kim further argues:

> North Korea's dilemma is that while pragmatic reform threatens the fundamental basis of its existence, change of policy will not produce the required economic improvement unless it is accompanied by change of system. This is the lesson of Gorbachev's failure . . . North Korea is bound to see its economy worsen. Given this situation, there is a real possibility that Kim Jong Il may find himself on the way out in the next few years, pushed out by reformists or military hard-liners. More likely, if he is forced out it will be a coalition

of different elements who will be united in one thing only:   the
judgment that Kim Jong Il is incompetent.[20]

Thus, the logic of a soft landing assumes that Pyongyang would be
able to enact meaningful economic reforms without endangering
regime stability.  In subsequent stages, the regime would presumably
modify its strategic objectives vis-à-vis the South by committing itself
to an enduring confidence-building measure (CBM) regime.  Thus,
discussions and negotiations with the United States and Japan would
not preclude greatly expanded interactions with the South, even as
the bedrock of North Korean ideology—*juche* and Kim Il Sungism—
was retained.  But the political costs associated with implementing
even portions of this overarching strategy are very likely to prove
prohibitive, and they run counter to the most basic tenets of the
North Korean state.  So long as the military serves as the backbone of
the Kim Jong Il regime and military capability is viewed as crucial to
the regime's survival strategy, it remains highly doubtful whether
North Korea will ever seriously contemplate wide-ranging economic
reforms.

An additional assumption underlying the soft-landing strategy is that
it offers the best chance for avoiding military conflict, even if pressures for political and economic change within North Korea increase.
Although North Korea retains a formidable military arsenal, the economic crisis, rising food shortages, and limited military assistance
from Russia and China have diminished its conventional combat capabilities.  But even as its economy further deteriorates, North Korea
continues to allocate disproportionate resources to development and
deployment of ballistic missiles, long-range artillery, weapons of
mass destruction, advanced munitions, and an upgraded command,
control, and communication system.  Thus, although traditional
concepts of deterrence and defense retain relevance in constraining
North Korean military options against the South, they are no longer
sufficient under all circumstances.  For example, if Kim Jong Il were
ousted in a military coup, or if his influence were severely curtailed
by a more politically assertive military, North Korean army units
could undertake hugely destabilizing actions, including terrorist at-

---

[20]Kyung Won Kim, "No Way Out:  North Korea's Impending Collapse," *Harvard
International Review,* Vol. 18, No. 2, Spring 1996, p. 24.

tacks against the South or other variants of low-intensity conflict. Under more desperate or potentially chaotic circumstances, outcomes become possible that do not apply under conditions of effective central control. It is against such possibilities that the United States and South Korea must increasingly prepare.

## EXPLAINING UNIFICATION SCENARIOS

As noted previously, before the German reunification in 1990, very little attention was paid to the mechanics or process of Korean unification. Even now, thinking about unification in South Korea continues to emphasize unification *formulas* rather than evaluating how unification could occur under different scenarios. In other words, there is considerable attention placed on how unification *should* be achieved, rather than on the *process* of unification and on major problems that could arise during this process. Depending on the context in which various political, economic, and military events occur, unification could occur with little early warning, or it could be postponed for years or decades. Hence, the goal in examining contrasting unification scenarios is to understand how unification could unfold, and the range of issues that could arise for the U.S. Army.

Toward this end, in this study we assess four principal scenarios:

- Unification through peaceful integration and negotiation;

- Unification through absorption following a collapse;

- Unification through conflict or war; and

- Sustained disequilibrium and potential external intervention.

It should be emphasized that these four scenarios do not constitute an exhaustive set of possibilities, nor will we offer predictions about the likelihood of specific outcomes. We have posited for analytic purposes specific time periods for this assessment (the present and the years 2000, 2005, and 2010). In light of our larger estimation of North Korean internal vulnerabilities, we believe these dates are wholly plausible.

A number of different permutations or variations can be considered under each of the scenarios, and some are examined in subsequent chapters for their strategic and operational implications.  For example, China is very likely to assume an important role in all four scenarios, given its long-standing relationship with the DPRK and its growing ties with the ROK.  Assuming that the South Korean government emerges as the successor government for the entire peninsula and that some U.S. forces remain deployed on the peninsula, the dissolution of the North Korean "buffer zone" could pose new security challenges for China and for Russia.  Major-power relations could undergo major stress and potential change once the momentum toward unification begins to accelerate.  It is beyond the scope of this study to explore these possibilities in detail, but we will assess particular scenarios according to four considerations:  (1) major characteristics, (2) potential indicators, (3) preferred and variant paths, and (4) strategic implications, including future regional geopolitics.

It is also useful to note the context in which the scenarios are considered.  Four distinct stages are posited on the road to unification.  In the "standby" stage, primary emphasis is placed on augmenting U.S. and ROK capabilities as they relate to the four basic scenarios.  Particular attention is given to early warning, intelligence assessment, critical indicators (both military and nonmilitary), and capabilities augmentation.  In the "trigger" stage, the scenarios sharpen based on various triggering events in North Korea or an external event that could act as a catalyst for accelerated change in North Korea.  For instance, a military coup in North Korea, massive refugee flows into China, South Korea, the Russian Far East, and Japan, a major military incident, or the sudden death of Kim Jong Il would stimulate a chain of highly disruptive consequences; indeed, any of these events by itself would prove highly destabilizing.  Benign stimuli could also be considered, including a South-North summit, successful completion of the four-party talks and signing of a permanent peace treaty to replace the armistice agreement, or a decision by the two Koreas to enact wide-ranging CBMs, including major force reductions.  In the "transition" stage, the relevant scenario is increasingly defined by specific political and military actions.  For example, the operational requirements for military forces would be most evident at this stage.  This stage, however, also takes into account the possibility of abrupt, unexpected developments (what we term deviant scenarios) that could pose major new operational requirements and constraints.  In the "outcome" stage, various preferred, alternative, or worst-case outcomes emerge fully.

All four scenarios could progress in either linear or discontinuous fashion. The specific sequence would likely depend on the magnitude and character of different triggering events. The predominant pattern would be differentiated by four main elements: (1) the degree of "structural integrity" of North Korea; (2) the political and military constraints affecting U.S.-ROK response options; (3) the types of forces and capabilities to be employed in each scenario; and (4) the desired political outcomes. But "unfamiliar" or "unconventional" transitions could also occur. These unanticipated outcomes could complicate or confound U.S. and ROK policy objectives and planning assumptions—for example, a North Korea that survives its present economic difficulties and is able to regain its strength and retain its strategic orientation. Alternatively, North Korea could "muddle through" its mounting economic difficulties but in the process lose its grip on its command and control system, with major implications for its ability to fully control all its armed forces or weapon systems. There could also be an acceleration of events with rapid escalatory potential, such as a military coup, civil uprising, and harsh crackdowns as a precursor of potential civil war and massive refugee flows. Moreover, ROK and U.S. response options could be inhibited by a range of political or military constraints, such as North Korea's use or threatened use of weapons of mass destruction or unilateral Chinese actions in response to an impending North Korean collapse or to ROK-U.S. entry into North Korea following a collapse. Finally, crisis planning and military operations could be disrupted by political discord among allies, including major disagreements over political objectives, intelligence assessments, and transit/access rights.

It is now necessary to turn to each scenario and its potential permutations.

# Chapter Three

# SCENARIO 1: INTEGRATION AND PEACEFUL UNIFICATION

The predominant focus in scenarios for the peninsula presumes an incremental transition in the North that enables increasing economic, social, and (ultimately) political interactions between South and North. Though many of the renderings of such a scenario seem formulaic and overly conceptual, there is a clear need to specify the policy and operational mechanisms needed to achieve major breakthroughs and ultimately produce national integration without a resort to force.

## MAJOR CHARACTERISTICS

For the ROK and the four major powers, peaceful unification through gradual integration, implementation of confidence-building measures and major threat reduction activities, and comprehensive political and social reconciliation between the two Koreas is the preferred unification option. For our purposes, we need to identify what such a process would entail.

We acknowledge at the outset that there is a necessary artificiality and implausibility to such a scenario, given that it is starkly contradicted by the acute ideological, political, and security animosities in place for a half century. Integration and peaceful unification also assumes that both South and North can overcome and forgo the zero-sum thinking they have held to almost constantly for this entire period. Thus, the scenario clearly posits two fundamental assumptions: (1) that both governments (and public opinion in the South) will undertake profound changes in attitudes and assumptions about each other and (2) that a series of interim steps can be instituted that ultimately allow the far larger changes posited under this model. Without meeting these two conditions, it is virtually impossible to imagine how the two sides would get from here to there. But given the major attention that peaceful unification continues to receive in various policy pronouncements and analytic assessments, it warrants careful description and evaluation.

Peaceful unification presumes the cessation of military threat, armed hostilities, and ideological antagonisms, ultimately enabling the creation of a unified Korean state. The process of integration between the two Koreas further assumes a political understanding or *modus vivendi,* including agreement on a permanent peace mechanism as an interim measure prior to formal unification. Though such an outcome clashes sharply with the realities of the peninsula today, both governments are familiar with its content and logic. The leaders of South and North first subscribed to some of these tenets in the "July 4 Joint Communiqué" of 1972. Subsequent measures paralleling or extending the logic of this accord included the December 12, 1991 Basic Agreement—the most comprehensive CBM ever concluded between the two Koreas—and the Joint South-North Declaration on the Denuclearization of the Korean Peninsula of January 20, 1992.[1] The common political requirement in all such documents is that both sides must agree to and implement comprehensive political arrangements that would supplant the half-century pattern of confrontation and hostility.

Toward these ends, both states would be obligated to agree to far-reaching military CBMs, ultimately enabling creation of an integrated military system between South and North. Peaceful unification also assumes economic integration that would build on pre-

---

[1]The formal title of the December 1991 accord is the "South-North Agreement on Reconciliation, Non-Aggression, and Exchange and Cooperation." It officially entered into force on February 19, 1992. The January 1992 denuclearization declaration forbids experimentation, manufacturing, production, acceptance, possession, storage, or use of nuclear weapons. It further states that the two sides will use nuclear energy only for peaceful purposes and that neither the South nor the North will possess a reprocessing or enrichment plant. For a compilation of important South-North agreements, see *Tongil Baekso* [Unification White Paper] (Seoul:  Ministry of Unification, 1996). For an English-language text, see *Peace and Cooperation—White Paper on Korean Unification* (Seoul:  Ministry of National Unification, Republic of Korea, 1996).

sumed complementarities between the two economies.[2] In addition, unification would necessitate a comprehensive redrafting of various international agreements and diplomatic documents. A successor state, for example, would need to renegotiate the entire spectrum of accords previously signed by the two Koreas, including the U.S.-ROK Mutual Defense Treaty, the DPRK's Treaty of Alliance and Mutual Assistance with China, and the North's Treaty of Friendship and Cooperation with Russia. These processes of change and rene-gotiation of different international agreements would undoubtedly be lengthy and complex.

Other dimensions of reconciliation would prove highly contentious. Resolution of past disputes, for example, would likely have to extend to assessing responsibility for the outbreak of the Korean War and terrorist acts committed by the North against the South (for example, the Rangoon bombing of 1983 and the bombing of a Korean Air Lines jet in 1987). Though some observers would see the need to set aside such hugely contentious historical issues for the larger purpose of national reconciliation, it is highly doubtful that they could be indef-initely deferred.

Assuming that peaceful negotiated unification occurs, the process would, at a minimum, encompass the following components:

**Political.** The South and the North would have to accept each other as full negotiating partners and as equal legal entities before com-mencing a series of negotiations that would lead to a mutually bind-ing political settlement. All of the current inter-Korean dialogue channels could be used, or an entirely new framework of communi-cations and negotiations could be established. In addition, general and specific principles and procedures would have to be enunciated, including the pace of negotiations, the desirability of gradual integra-tion between the two sides, and specific norms to govern political relations.

---

[2]An in-depth treatment of unification is provided by Sung Chul Yang, *The North and South Korean Political Systems* (Seoul: Westview Press and Seoul Press, 1994). Yang offers a comprehensive review of the economic history of the South and the North, including the relative performance of both systems and the challenges to economic cooperation.

**Legal.** The South and the North would have to draft new laws, regulations, and agreements to enable negotiations on a comprehensive structure that covers all aspects of unified governance.

**Security.** The 1953 armistice agreement signed between the United States (as head of the United Nations Forces), China, and North Korea would have to be replaced by a permanent peace treaty. A mechanism for collaboration between the militaries of both systems would have to be enunciated before any steps toward integration could proceed. The question of the future of the United Nations Command, the Combined Forces Command, and other subcommands would have to be addressed as well. As mentioned above, North Korea's military agreements with China and Russia would also require careful review prior to formal unification talks.

## POTENTIAL INDICATORS

Many of the indicators of peaceful unification would be self-evident, including routinized political exchanges and summit meetings; ad-

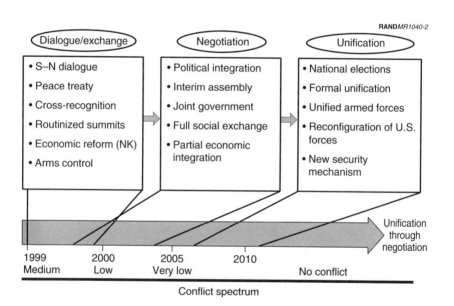

Figure 2—Integration and Unification

herence to already signed South-North accords such as the 1991 Basic Agreement; implementation of a mutually verifiable CBM regime; unhindered construction of the light-water reactors under KEDO; and full compliance by North Korea and the United States with the October 1994 Agreed Framework.  Other functional indicators would attest to a fairly high degree of predictability that assumes productive negotiations between the two Koreas.  We have outlined these below.

## Political Indicators

- Mutual recognition across political institutions.
- Cessation of all political propaganda by both sides.
- Routinized high-level exchanges, including summit meetings.
- Release of all political prisoners in North and South.
- Abrogation of national security and espionage laws (as they apply to the two Koreas).
- Extensive exchanges between political parties.
- Ability to engage in political activities in the South and North.

## Social and Economic Indicators

- More freedom of movement and travel within and between the two Koreas, as well as abroad.
- Cessation of government censorship.
- Removal of restrictions on dissemination of print and electronic media.
- Ability to enroll freely in schools and educational institutions.
- Decoupling of economic exchanges from reciprocal political measures.
- Constitutional and legislative changes that allow for unconstrained economic activities between the South and the North, including the flow of people, goods, services, capital, and technologies.

- Upgrading of joint venture laws in the North.

- Full convertibility of the currencies of South and North.

## Military and Security Indicators

- Unconditional North Korean participation in the four-party talks.

- Cessation of diplomatic competition between the two Koreas and establishment of diplomatic ties between the United States and North Korea and Japan and North Korea.

- Replacement of the Armistice Agreement (1953) with a permanent peace treaty.

- Maintenance of all KEDO provisions and conditions.

- Full North Korean compliance with International Atomic Energy Agency (IAEA) and NPT provisions.

- Significant progress in military CBMs, including prenotification of military exercises, establishment of a military hotline, mutual observation of military exercises and other command post exercises, and step-by-step, fully verifiable force reductions.

- Cessation of all military activities construed as provocative or offensive.

It is difficult to imagine that all of these indicators would appear before peaceful unification, given that many of them imply profound changes for both Koreas but especially North Korea. Indeed, the question of more practical, interim measures still remains. Many, if not all, of these indicators would entail a substantial level of negotiation and prior agreement between the Koreas. The major distinguishing characteristic of the peaceful unification scenario compared to other scenarios is that *agreement and compliance must be in place before, during, and after unification and that agreement must be reached at all levels of both systems in order to create a functioning, unified government.* This last requirement is probably the most difficult part of the peaceful unification scenario. The two Koreas not only have to come to terms politically at the highest level, but mutual confidence and agreement must be reached at all other levels before creating a unified government. An additional important requirement for peaceful unification is the generation of strong public support. Various unification proposals, such as the "National Commonwealth" model of the early 1990s and Kim Dae Jung's calls for realizing "co-existence and co-prosperity," presume interim steps that would enable mutual accommodation and integration prior to unification. Thus, peaceful unification would entail a fundamental political and strategic transformation within and between both governments, and in the populations of South and North.

## VARIATIONS

One of the more problematic dimensions of the peaceful unification scenario is that it could fail if there are major deviations in concept or operation. Negotiation between the two Koreas is likely to be a protracted, uneven process. Moreover, the creation of a credible negotiating context presumes extensive reform in the North. But the prospects for such reform, at least in relation to the Kim Jong Il regime, remain highly improbable.

Thus, deviations or unexpected outcomes in the peaceful unification scenario could occur in any of its stages or dimensions. For example, unless and until the DPRK accepts the ROK as a full political partner (and vice versa), there will be little realistic progress in implementing CBM provisions contained in the Basic Agreement. In the security realm, the peaceful unification scenario also assumes that the North will choose to drop its decades-long demand for the withdrawal of U.S. forces from the ROK, and that the two Koreas will be able to come to terms with respect to the deployment of U.S. forces after unification. Conversely, a unified Korean government could decide to terminate all U.S. military deployments on the peninsula, or agree to a substantially smaller U.S. military presence.

## Table 1

### Peaceful Unification: Preferred and Alternative Paths

| Preferred Path | Indicators | Possible Outcomes | Potential Implications |
|---|---|---|---|
| Unconditional NK participation in four-party talks | No linkage with food aid, U.S. troop withdrawals | Diplomatic normalization with U.S./Japan | Stability in NK and in South-North relations |
| | Full talks with SK | Full-scale CBMs | U.S. force reductions or withdrawal |
| | Extensive arms control and CBMs | | |
| **Alternative Paths** | | | |
| Cessation of or stonewalling in negotiations | Linkage of food aid with U.S. troop withdrawals | Intermittent relations with U.S., Japan, but no firm deal with SK | Rise of military in NK, dithering and delay in four-party talks |
| Scrapping or undermining of nuclear agreement | Reduced cooperation with IAEA, continued missile sales, new military cooperation with Russia, no additional assistance on MIA | Threatened NK withdrawal from NPT, IAEA | Increased possibility of negotiating breakdown |

# Chapter Four

# SCENARIO 2: COLLAPSE AND ABSORPTION

As discussed previously, German unification, the collapse of communist regimes across Eastern and Central Europe, and the dissolution of the Soviet Union prompted a surge of interest in the possibility of a similar chain of events in North Korea. A collapse could indeed occur, but how such a process would unfold, the types of events that could trigger it, and its operational consequences remain widely contested. Although the German model provides a useful historical analogy, there are a number of differences between the collapse of East Germany and a potential collapse of North Korea. Unlike the two Germanys, the two Koreas fought a bitter and bloody war from 1950 to 1953 that produced a stark and sustained confrontation on the peninsula. Although West Germany faced a military threat from the East, this was embedded in the larger NATO–Warsaw Pact rivalry, rather than a "stand-alone" East German military threat. Indeed, the two Germanys agreed to simultaneous recognition in 1972, thereby permitting full diplomatic relations and a quasi-normal political relationship for nearly two decades before unification.

In the Korean case, there has been barely a semblance of regular contact in any major realm—political, institutional, diplomatic, economic, or social—for a full half century. At least as important, the internal vulnerabilities in the North, in conjunction with the extraordinary array of weaponry and military forces controlled by leaders in Pyongyang, create major potential for various forms of armed conflict. When the East German ruling structure collapsed in 1990, the possibility of any armed hostilities between the Warsaw Pact and NATO had virtually ceased. This is simply not the case in

North Korea. Thus, any loss of central control in the North would create inherent risks of armed conflict, either within or across the North's borders. This would almost certainly find U.S. Army units immediately involved in any resultant hostilities.

It is also important to note the nature of the regime in power in North Korea, as compared to that in East Germany. Though the East German authorities sought to penetrate and undermine the government in the West, unification through military means was never a central component of East German strategy. For added measure, the East German military establishment—even at the peak of its capabilities—could not have operated independent of Soviet command and control. By comparison, even a weakened North Korea retains a capacity for autonomous action, and it has deployed the bulk of its military forces close to the ROK's borders for precisely these purposes.

A more apt comparison to North Korea is not East Germany (notwithstanding the implications for unification in the two cases) but Romania. Romania under Ceausescu and North Korea under Kim Il Sung and Kim Jong Il bear ample resemblance. Both regimes possess(ed) comparable attributes—i.e., personalism and familial dominance in the extreme, including absolutism, an unchallenged cult of personality, and a pervasive internal security and surveillance apparatus.[1] When the central leadership in Romania fractured, the veneer of stability atop the system was shattered, leading to the execution of Ceausescu and a rapid collapse of party and army authority.

Kim Jong Il has clearly gone to extraordinary lengths to prevent such a possibility, in part by relying on extreme secrecy and infrequent public appearances. Should a comparable sequence of events nonetheless unfold in the North, the risks would be incomparably greater, given the array of military capabilities and the implications if the command system were either "headless" or subject to rival power claims. For example, if the Korean People's Army (KPA) leadership

---

[1]For an especially evocative account of the control mechanisms surrounding the Kim Jong Il regime, see the interview conducted by Olaf Jahn with high-level North Korean defector Hwang Jang Yop, published in *Far Eastern Economic Review*, October 15, 1998, pp. 30, 32.

fractured and left no effective central control, the North Korean military could divide into rival units, each having political and territorial control over specific areas of the country, and each with control over particular weapons systems. This situation would carry an inherent risk of internal violence, with the latent potential for spillover consequences. For these reasons alone, the collapse scenario warrants close consideration.

## MAJOR CHARACTERISTICS

As noted previously, we have defined collapse (i.e., the hard landing scenario) as the inability of the regime in power to maintain effective political, economic, social, and military control, which ultimately leads to its dissolution and, in the extreme case, the formal end of the state. Three variations could also be considered: (1) a collapse that results in dissolution of the ruling regime, with a successor regime managing to retain political and military control; (2) a collapse where political instability is rampant and where the successor regime is unable to establish or retain effective governing authority led either by the party, the bureaucracy, or the military; and (3) a collapse that could precipitate some type of conflict—internally in the form of limited military clashes with existing governing authorities or externally in terms of border clashes with the South or more extensive military operations directed against the ROK. That said, the conditions under which North Korea could collapse are difficult to predict. Though the defining context might be economic, the precipitating factor (as with Romania) would very likely be political (i.e., conflict within the leadership). Thus, if North Korea's economic crisis is not reversed, members of the elite who saw the system's survival at stake might seek Kim's ouster, though this would be a hugely risky proposition. This counter-elite could include "reformers" if the term is taken to mean members of the *nomenklatura* who (although not eager to dismantle key institutions of the DPRK) ultimately conclude that Kim Jong Il is simply unwilling and unable to undertake meaningful economic change, given that his legitimacy appears to depend on unquestioned fidelity to the policies of his father.

The North Korean economy may be able to limp along for a few more years, but it is unlikely to realize any appreciable recovery. Under such circumstances, Kim Jong Il would be progressively less able to guarantee even a minimal livelihood for ever-larger portions of the population, including an expanding number of those within ruling elites and their families.  The counterargument, however, is that North Koreans have always lived under stark economic conditions.  Though this is undeniably true, overall economic conditions have worsened sharply under Kim Jong Il and have very likely affected ever-increasing numbers of party and military cadres.  Thus, the greatest dangers to regime stability, if not its survival, are the growing pressure for more flexible policies to permit a degree of economic recovery and an improvement in people's livelihood, and the risk that political and personal loyalties to Kim Jong Il might erode.  At the same time, because Kim Jong Il depends heavily on military support for his survival, he must continue to pour scarce resources into the defense sector, compounding the problems of the system as a whole.  But the country's larger economic decline has almost certainly impinged on military well-being, though it is hurting proportionately less than other institutions.

Thus, if a collapse occurs in the North, the catalyst will most likely be acute disaffection or pressures for change from somewhere (or someone) atop the system.  So construed, a deteriorating economy is a necessary but not sufficient condition for a collapse.  But assessing the political fortunes of the Kim Jong Il regime is hugely challenging.  To most appearances, Kim has consolidated his absolute grasp on power atop the system, and it is difficult to identify who in the power structure might opt to challenge him, given the long odds.  This said, North Korea is clearly a system under great and growing stress.  For example, during the decade of the 1980s, the total number of defectors was 49; this number more than doubled in the ensuing half decade, including increased numbers of individuals who had occupied fairly high positions in the *nomenklatura*.[2]

The most celebrated case occurred in February 1997, when Hwang Jang Yop, a member of the KWP Central Committee and its long-time secretary for international affairs, defected to the ROK while on a visit to Beijing.  Though Hwang's defection was a major propaganda boon for the ROK and a comparable setback to the DPRK, it did not

---

[2]Shim Jae Hoon, "The Image Cracks," *Far Eastern Economic Review*, February 29, 1996, p. 15.

appear to trigger any fundamental changes in leadership atop the system. In various interviews since his defection, Hwang has offered numerous controversial judgments (for example, he claimed that significant numbers of South Koreans from all walks of life had long collaborated with the North) and has further asserted that the North has a limited number of nuclear weapons and is prepared to attack the ROK should U.S. forces ever withdraw from the peninsula.[3] Though additional defections followed Hwang's (including the North Korean ambassador to Egypt, his wife, and his brother, all in August 1997), neither the South Korean nor the U.S. governments deemed such events precursors to collapse.[4] Indeed, Hwang's defection may reflect generational considerations, given that his principal ties (Hwang is 75) were to Kim Il Sung and his coterie, not to Kim Jong Il. But such developments do not reflect a healthy system, and over time, pressures on the core elite seem certain to mount.

Though many observers assert that North Korea (like the Soviet Union under Gorbachev and China under Deng Xiaoping) will ultimately conclude that major reform is both inevitable and desirable, Kim Jong Il and his inner circle very likely view these historical examples as fraught with major risk. The subsequent collapse of the USSR is hardly an endorsement for the virtues and benefits of a North Korean–style *perestroika*. And China's pursuit of an economically driven foreign and domestic policy has unleashed societal changes that are assuredly anathema to Kim and his principal lieutenants. For good measure, pursuit of any "Chinese style reform"—a policy that among its other liabilities to Pyongyang led inexorably to a large-scale China-ROK trade and investment relationship—would very likely find the North Korean leadership under the increasing sway of leaders in Beijing. For the time being, Pyongyang will try to buy time through negotiations with the United States and Japan in the hope of receiving much-needed economic assistance. Over the next several years, North Korea has little choice but to hunker down domestically and ride out its economic difficulties. But as the

---

[3]See, for example, Kevin Sullivan, "Key Defector Warns Again of North Korean War Plans," *Washington Post*, July 10, 1997; and "Running Against History," op cit.

[4]See the comments of State Department spokesman James Rubin, as cited in Jane A. Morse, "North Korean Ambassador Defects to the United States," *USIS Washington File*, August 26, 1997, p. 1.

regime's strategic options narrow and as maintaining the status quo becomes more costly, pressures will assuredly mount within the system. Corrective measures may well be taken to alleviate acute shortages, but more comprehensive reform will be far less tenable.

Though a range of options are conceivable (at least in hypothetical terms), North Korea's central dilemma is that a fundamental transformation can occur only in the context of a sweeping regime change. The current leadership under Kim Jong Il is extremely unlikely to choose such a path. The acid test for North Korea will come when all its other policy options are exhausted, and systemic atrophy reaches unmanageable levels. Then the regime will face its most profound challenge since 1948. Therefore, far-reaching change on the Korean peninsula can only materialize in the aftermath of a substantial departure from the status quo in North Korea. Active crisis management and attendant policy responses on the part of South Korea and the United States will commence from that point.

## POTENTIAL INDICATORS

Indicators that predict to an imminent major political or military crisis in the North could be quite limited. The closed nature of the system, the lack of independent means to verify critical pieces of information (or even rumors), and reliance on defectors' possibly outdated testimony mean that if a regime collapse occurs, the outside world may have very little warning. That said, even a system as closed as North Korea's has certain functional characteristics, and given that political and military power is highly personalized and concentrated, certain signals could be likely precursors to more ominous developments.

### Political Indicators

- Increased defections to South Korea, China, and Russia of high-ranking North Korean officials and military officers.

- Sudden shifts in the leadership hierarchy, such as the Politburo, the Central Committee of the KWP, and the Central Military Commission.

RAND*MR1040-3*

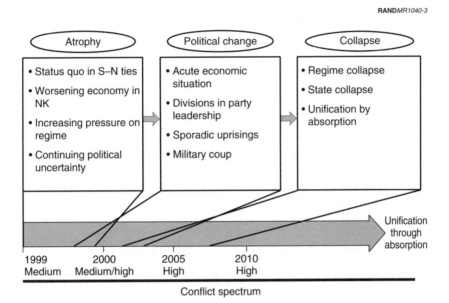

Figure 3—Collapse and Absorption

- Prolonged absence from public view of key government, party, and military personnel.

- Oblique criticism of Kim Jong Il's rule and legitimacy in the official media (e.g., reports on foreign political developments with certain similarities).

- Downgrading of party activities and anniversaries.

## Socioeconomic Indicators

- Final breakdown of the ration system, i.e., lifting of all travel permit requirements to secure food supplies.

- Continued declines in grain harvests and increasing requests for food and related humanitarian assistance.

- A major surge in refugee flows into China, the Russian Far East, and South Korea.

- Increased crackdown on "antisocialist crimes," including official corruption, "hooliganism," prostitution, and petty theft.
- Growing incidence of public executions.
- Increased transfer of internal security duties from the Ministry of State Security to army units.
- Increased surveillance of "wavering" and "hostile" classes.

## Military and Security Indicators

- Growing militarization of the party through allotment of key party posts to senior military officers.
- Rigidification of major foreign policy positions.
- Unexpected or unusual military appointments.
- Withdrawal from four-party talks.
- Unilateral suspension of the Agreed Framework.
- Discontinuation of KEDO.
- No participation in normalization talks with the United States and Japan.
- Withdrawal from negotiations pertaining to counterproliferation and the MIA issue.

## VARIATIONS

Depending on the nature of regime collapse in North Korea, several permutations or variations could occur. If a group of military officers decides to oust Kim Jong Il through a coup, the conspirators would have the option of installing another member of the Kim family, such as half-brother Kim Pyung Il, as the new leader. Alternatively, the military could seek to remove all members of the extended Kim family who have assumed key posts throughout the party, the bureaucracy, and intelligence apparatus. However, the important point is not whether the successor government will be led by the military, the party, or a coalition comprising leaders from the party and the military. The main issue is whether the successor government will be able to (1) retain power and loyalty throughout the system, (2) enact economic reforms, (3) assert effective domestic control, and (4) maintain control over major military assets. However, a desire for economic reform need not be a catalyst for removing Kim Jong Il from power. If remnants of the KPA leadership decide to pool their resources to oust Kim, they could be working under a number of different motivations. Despite the extremely tight control that Kim Jong Il exercises over the armed forces, for example, senior officers could resent his lack of real military experience and his promotion of officers based primarily on loyalty and homage to Kim, rather than professional military or command skills. Unconfirmed reports of purges within the armed forces, if true, could reflect disaffection and discontent within various military units, and such disgruntlement could prove decisive in a potential coup.

An additional question is whether a successor regime would be able to retain effective control without rectifying the all-important food shortage problem. Although the KPA continues to receive preferential treatment in terms of grain supplies and other provisions, the near-famine of the last several years has also affected military units. Thus, the successor regime would have to enact reform measures to bring about meaningful economic improvements and at least a partial alleviation of extreme shortages of food and other essentials. If a successor regime fails to devise credible economic response options and continues to run the country by simply proffering scarce resources to an alternative leadership group, popular discontent could quickly begin to surface, including protests in key urban centers. If the government, run by either a collective leadership or a military junta, opts to quell all forms of dissent by even harsher crackdowns, open demonstrations against the regime and even the possibility of internal violence can no longer be discounted.[5]

This scenario and its variants amply underscore the powerful incentives of North Korea's neighbors to see the manifestations of instability contained within the North's borders. Under circumstances where events might lurch simultaneously in contradictory directions and where intelligence indicators were inconclusive or subject to di-

---

[5]See, for instance, Yong-Sup Han, "The Kim Jong Il Regime's Strategic Choices and South Korea's Response," *IRI Review,* Vol. 1, No. 1, Spring 1996, p. 51.

vergent interpretation, external response options could also vary. For example, as indications of internal upheaval mounted (including the possibility of armed violence), individuals from abroad residing in the North (including NGO representatives and South Koreans involved in the KEDO process) could be hugely at risk, or they might be taken hostage by rival forces. The very fact that such individuals could confront personal danger might compel neighboring governments—including both the ROK and China—to react. Indeed, even in the absence of compelling evidence that internal violence might spread outward, CFC would undoubtedly have initiated a variety of precautionary and preparatory measures to forestall ever more dangerous possibilities. To consider one such prospect, we need to turn attention to our third scenario.

**Table 2**

**Collapse and Absorption:  Preferred and Alternative Paths**

| Preferred Path | Indicators | Possible Outcomes | Implications |
|---|---|---|---|
| Army retains control, undertakes initial economic reforms | Ouster of Kim Jong Il and direct military rule | Sustaining of NK regime under military auspices | Stabilized NK, renewed focus on economic development |
| Alternative Paths | | | |
| Major clash between army and party | Signals in official media, rapid turnover in leadership, military coup | Military crackdown; internal power struggle | Prolonged political turmoil, mounting signs of internal instability |
| De facto military rule with ultra-conservative outlook | Renewed threats to withdraw from NPT, discontinue KEDO work; break off talks with U.S., Japan, ROK | Restart nuclear weapons program, accelerate war preparations | Increased risk of destabilized military balance |

# Chapter Five

# SCENARIO 3: UNIFICATION THROUGH CONFLICT

Despite widespread evidence of systemic decline and even as the South endeavors to close the gap in various military capabilities, North Korea continues to invest heavily in major force modernization programs such as ballistic missiles, long-range artillery, advanced munitions, and upgraded command, control, and communication ($C^3I$) systems.[1] While the threat of a major conventional conflict comparable to the Korean War cannot be dismissed, and although North Korea's WMD capabilities—including its potential nuclear weapons capability—add an ominous new dimension to threat dynamics on the peninsula, the possibility of a massive assault would seem to have receded. For what purposes, then, does North Korea maintain a standing army of more than one million soldiers? And what do such capabilities portend in the event of an internal crisis?

## MAJOR CHARACTERISTICS

Despite North Korea's hugely problematic economic prospects, its principal military objectives appear to have changed very little during the 1990s: (1) maintain the military capabilities needed to achieve strategic and operational surprise in wartime and to sustain strategic momentum so that breakthrough operations can be successfully concluded before the arrival of major U.S. reinforcements; (2) utilize massive firepower against CFC forces through its artillery,

---

[1] *Strategic Assessment 1997* (Washington, D.C.: Institute for National Strategic Studies, National Defense University, 1997), pp. 100–101.

multiple rocket launchers, and surface-to-surface missiles; (3) isolate Seoul and capture all air and naval facilities capable of supporting U.S. reinforcement and resupply efforts; (4) neutralize ROK and U.S. air power; and (5) foster widespread internal confusion and panic in the population of the South, thereby creating domestic pressures in the ROK for a settlement on terms advantageous to the DPRK.

A robust military arsenal, especially WMD capabilities, also allows North Korea to diminish its sense of strategic vulnerability stemming from the growing disparity between the North's dwindling economic assets and the South's economic capabilities and from its inability to weaken the U.S.-ROK alliance.  But if North Korea introduces nuclear, biological, or chemical weapons during a conflict or threatens to employ them for specific political or military purposes in a crisis, this would activate massive responses by CFC.  For Pyongyang, the key operational imperative if an initial breakthrough were nonetheless achieved would be to deter, delay, or otherwise neutralize the effectiveness of U.S. reinforcements.  Indeed, in a second Korean conflict, the North may believe that the strategic center of gravity is not the Seoul region, but rather the airports and seaports well below Seoul.  Threatened or outright use of WMD capabilities, irrespective of the risks or consequences, might therefore be seen as critical to advancing vital North Korean political and military objectives.

How would CFC respond to any such attacks?  Bound by international treaties not to use biological or chemical weapons, the United States and South Korea would need to weigh and implement alternative response options.  CFC could consider an array of denial or punishment alternatives, including preemptive strikes at various targets in the North; or if the North used nuclear weapons against the South, the United States would need to weigh the costs and risks of a proportional nuclear response.  The United States could also opt to launch comprehensive strikes against key C$^3$I and WMD storage areas.  But many analysts express serious doubts about the military utility of such retaliatory strikes, which could entail substantial political repercussions and might also trigger military moves by China.  Indeed, if North Korea convinces the United States and the ROK that major retaliatory strikes are not a viable military option, it could pressure the South into ending hostilities in the North's favor.

North Korea could also consider destabilization campaigns against the South without resorting to full-scale war. For example, psychological operations could be tailored to specific targets in South Korea and perhaps even in a third country such as Japan. Support for radical student movements through discreet financial support; polarization of public attitudes on unification and security (such as the status of U.S. forces); and disinformation campaigns through the media could all be considered. The North could also resort to renewed terrorist campaigns, as evinced by the Rangoon bombing of 1983 and the downing of a South Korean passenger jet in 1987. Notwithstanding the greater opportunities for such actions under a democratic and more open South Korea, it remains doubtful that these operations would yield their desired political effects within South Korea, and might even provoke a stiffening of public opinion and calls for reprisals against the North. A more relevant possibility is for the North to embark on a series of incursions, including renewed efforts to undermine the Armistice Agreement and ad hoc missions akin to the submarine infiltration incidents of September 1996 and June 1998. For instance, more than 100 North Korean troops entered the northern sector of the Joint Security Area (JSA) at Panmunjom on April 6, 1996, a day after North Korea announced it had "dismissed" the armistice with the South.[2] Both ROK and U.S. forces were put on a higher state of alert—Watchcon 2—although there was no change in defense readiness, which was maintained at Defcon 4. (The CFC reverted to Watchcon 3 several weeks after the April armistice violation.)

In addition, North Korea could initiate conflict to achieve limited strategic aims. After Iraq's invasion of Kuwait in August 1990, the central strategic concern of the United States was that Saddam Hussein might launch a limited ballistic missile strike against Saudi Arabia and, after ensuring that its economic interests were satisfied, ultimately "withdraw" to its own border. If Iraq had withdrawn its forces from Kuwait just before the expiration of the UN Security Council's deadline for a peaceful resolution, it is highly unlikely that coalition forces would have launched their attack on Iraq, nor would the United States have been able to sustain the coalition if it attacked Iraq. Not only would Saddam have avoided costly economic sanc-

---

[2] *Korea Herald,* April 10, 1996.

tions, he would have achieved three strategic aims:   convincing Kuwait and Saudi Arabia that Iraq could *always* exercise a military option if diplomacy failed; retaining significant economic leverage by forcing concessions from Kuwait and Saudi Arabia; and breaking the coalition's political and military unity *without* any military cost. Moreover, there would have been no compelling reason for various U.S. allies to discontinue their robust trade relationship with Iraq once the dust had settled.  In comparable fashion, North Korea could opt to conduct war to achieve limited strategic aims, hoping that the attack itself might trigger a massive collapse of morale in the South, especially in Seoul.  If the North Koreans indicated that their objective was *not* to engage in a protracted war with U.S. forces, political pressure could mount in Washington to accept a peace settlement on terms favorable to the North.

## POTENTIAL INDICATORS

More than any other scenario, CFC has planned and trained for major military actions on the Korean peninsula, including a full-scale war launched against the ROK.  Thus, many of the indicators noted below very likely duplicate early-warning indicators monitored closely by CFC.  But some of the conditions that could result in the use of force or outbreak of conflict seem different from what they were several decades ago.  For instance, although the possibility of a massive North Korean attack can never be ignored, the strategic environment that permitted North Korea to launch the Korean War in 1950—a very weak South Korea, support from the Soviet Union and China, and an ambiguous U.S. security commitment to the ROK—no longer exists.  Therefore, the more relevant issue is to evaluate potential events or developments that could—either out of desperation or perhaps in a more deceptive military campaign—persuade the North to use force.

### Political Indicators

- Replacement of "technocrats" with hard-line senior military officers.

- Accusations and diplomatic *demarches* alleging ROK offensive actions directed against the North.

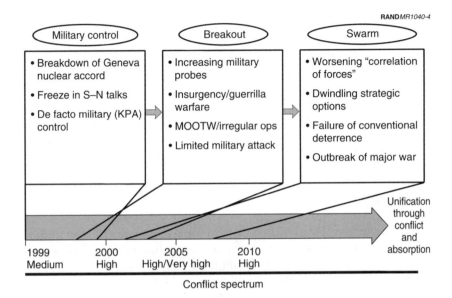

**Figure 4—Disequilibrium and Conflict**

- Primary emphasis on maintaining a war-footing economy.

- Exhortations by the top leadership to overcome economic difficulties through even greater ideological indoctrination.

- Propagating war preparations to maximize mobilization efforts.

## Socioeconomic Indicators

- Reinforcement of tight control over internal population movement.

- Enhanced surveillance of all citizens.

- Implementation of wartime rations.

- Reallocation of school and work units to key defense industries
military units, or paramilitary units.

## Military-Security Indicators

- Abrogation of the Agreed Framework.

- Accelerated training regimes for key military units.

- Increased activities of commando units.

- Increased North Korean activities, deployments in JSA.

- Increased activities around missile sites, including further deployments.

## VARIATIONS

As noted above, a North Korean use of force can be postulated under two principal circumstances. First, domestic instability in the North could precipitate political and military disintegration, which in turn could result in unauthorized applications of force or limited military probes by contending factions within the KPA (i.e., the collapse scenario). Second, Kim Jong Il could make an irrevocable decision—in essence, a strategic roll of the dice—to employ his military assets before they degrade further, to exploit South Korea's internal preoccupations, and to gain major political advantage for the North. In the latter case, however, Kim might seek to exploit the external *perception* of mounting instability and vulnerability in the North for advantage, or as a means to limit CFC responses. For example, North Korean officials or media might claim that specific actions taken by KPA units were independent of central policy guidance, thereby potentially delaying CFC responses. Alternatively, Kim could employ various threats (e.g., threatening to withdraw from KEDO in order to postpone nuclear inspections by the IAEA) as means to deflect external pressure, mobilize internal support, and (as in 1993–1994) caution the United States as to the potential consequences of any military moves against the North. Military preparedness and various shows of force could also be utilized in efforts to garner increased economic assistance to the North.

However, none of these factors is meant to imply that the North possesses a war-winning strategy. Indeed, absent strategic and operational surprise and a U.S.-ROK intelligence failure of staggering proportions, the prospects for North Korean "success" in either political or military terms would seem hugely problematic. This reflects both the highly diversified war plans and intelligence capabilities maintained by CFC, and the fact that the North would be acting independent of any support from either China or Russia. Indeed, the contrary case seems much more likely. The North Koreans would very likely go to ample lengths to obscure any impending military operations from their erstwhile allies, neither of whom has any conceivable incentive to encourage or support an unprovoked North Korean attack on the South. In the event that Pyongyang were to fail in these nondisclosure efforts (i.e., in relation to China, Russia, or both), Beijing or Moscow could seek to preempt an impending major crisis on the peninsula by major, high-level political pressure on the North, and simultaneous consultations with the ROK, United States, or both to inform them of impending North Korean actions.

Thus, execution of North Korean war plans would entail extraordinary risks, with a nonnegligible possibility that it could result in the end of the regime (or state) and unification on terms highly favorable to the ROK. But this fact does not render this scenario wholly implausible, especially under conditions of continued internal decline. In the final analysis, the calculations of Kim Jong Il and a very small circle of his closest subordinates, and Kim's personal calculation of gain, risk, and prospective consequences, will prove decisive. Anticipating and preparing for the full spectrum of outcomes that could emanate from this leadership must remain the fundamental priority of the United States, the ROK, and their military establishments.

# Chapter Six

# SCENARIO 4: DISEQUILIBRIUM AND POTENTIAL EXTERNAL INTERVENTION

The possible paths to Korean unification are highly varied and potentially discontinuous. Even among the three scenarios reviewed so far, deviations or variations could result in different outcomes or change the time frames of expected outcomes. No matter what the path to unification, however, the defense planner is unlikely to be caught completely by surprise. But the fourth scenario—an environment characterized by sustained disequilibrium but not necessarily chaos or collapse—could pose particularly vexing challenges for the U.S. Army. This scenario is dominated by events that lead to "gray outcomes," i.e., ambiguous political or military outcomes that are difficult to pinpoint or define. For example, if a regime collapse occurs in the North and a successor government is in power but unable to address daunting economic problems, how should the ROK and the United States deal with a weakened, but not collapsing, DPRK government? Alternatively, what are the implications if North Korea, on the verge of collapse, requests and receives political and military assistance from China? Assuming that China extends support to the North in addition to explicit signals that it will not remain passive in the event of impending meltdown in the North, what policy objectives should the United States and the ROK pursue?

## MAJOR CHARACTERISTICS

Among the permutations that seem possible under a gray outcome, we will focus on two, given their strategic and operational challenges. The first would be a "hollowed out" North Korea (i.e., a minimally functioning state that for all practical purposes seems on the edge of collapse).  A gravely weakened state in the North could nonetheless entail an array of worrisome consequences for the U.S. and ROK. The second, and strategically more consequential possibility, would entail the increased possibility of a Chinese intervention to forestall outright collapse.  This is not to predict that the Chinese are currently anticipating such an intervention, but that under certain conditions we cannot preclude the possibility.

At present, China is contributing more substantial food and energy aid to the North than it did during the first half of the 1990s, with Beijing and Pyongyang both making public reference to some of this assistance.  The assistance may also also result in a visit by Kim Jong Il to China, which leaders in Beijing have purportedly been pursuing for some time.[1]  We characterize this assistance as a prudent "life support" strategy not dissimilar from the assistance proffered by the United States, ROK, and various NGOs—i.e., aid that avoids a calamitous humanitarian outcome but is not on a scale likely to enable fuller economic recovery, especially if the latter prospect might also augment the North's military activities.  The question posed by this scenario, however, is whether there are circumstances that might lead the Chinese to undertake more heroic measures on behalf of a gravely weakened North.

There appear to be three circumstances under which China might weigh such a course of action:  (1) in the event that the North (despite a clear aversion to dependence on China) signals a readiness to "tilt" toward Beijing in exchange for enhanced economic and political support; (2) if the indicators of instability in the North and its possible repercussions for stability and security in contiguous border areas of China convince Beijing that it must act to protect its own interests; and (3) if the ROK and the United States were to embark on unilateral actions to counter instability in the North that Beijing believed would undermine China's long-term political and security interests.

From the perspective of China, a North Korea tottering on the brink of collapse would pose a major policy dilemma.  If the Chinese lead-

---

[1]Despite repeated claims that Kim will visit Beijing in the fall of 1999, there is no definitive confirmation of this possibility.  For one such claim, see "North Korea Chief Making First Trip to China," *The New York Times,* March 3, 1999.

ership decided that a North Korean collapse was inevitable and that despite historical ties it was not in China's interest to prolong the state's existence, Beijing would seek to contain the risks within the territory of the North and ensure its strategic and economic interests in a unified Korea under the auspices of the ROK. To enhance its potential political or diplomatic leverage, China would endeavor to dissuade the ROK and the United States from direct involvement in the North, and convey that if the DPRK collapses, the ROK and the United States should not deploy military personnel north of the 38th parallel. Alternatively, Beijing might opt to significantly accelerate its cooperation and communication with the United States and ROK, enabling all three states to manage an endgame crisis in the North, while simultaneously reducing the risk of misperception or an overt clash of interests among them. At a minimum, however, China would have to be prepared for four developments: (1) the potential for significant refugee flows into northeastern China; (2) the political and economic consequences of a unified Korea led by the ROK; (3) the possibility that the United States might continue to deploy forces on the peninsula after unification; and (4) the ramifications of a strong U.S.-Japan security relationship in addition to a robust U.S.-ROK alliance in the postunification era.

If the Chinese leadership nonetheless concludes that internal conditions in North Korea require increased attention and involvement, we should anticipate mounting Chinese expressions of concern over the plight of the North Korean regime and reference to various actions the North Koreans might take in desperation. China would also send increased signals of opposition to U.S.-ROK preemption or intervention in response to an internal North Korean crisis. Finally, if Beijing believes that North Korea's internal stability is in serious jeopardy, it could prudently begin to enhance its response capabilities, even as it would likely seek to minimize the potential negative consequences for Sino-American relations and Sino-ROK relations.

However, China does not necessarily face an "either-or" decision. For example, a commitment to maintain the North Korean system in power looks very different from one where Beijing was prudently preparing for instability that threatened to trigger a major humanitarian crisis along the Sino–North Korean border; precautionary measures to warn (or preempt) the United States and ROK from undertaking unilateral actions would also have a different dynamic.

Though the Chinese would have no incentives for their intentions to be misread, it is also possible that Beijing would want first to signal commitment by redeployment of some of its forces, but short of direct involvement in the North. Such a "virtual intervention," though it could complicate near-term U.S.-ROK response options, might constitute something of a holding pattern, as the Chinese sought to communicate more fully with U.S. and ROK officials. But prudent measures to enhance security along the border (case two) would also reflect augmented capability and commitment. As such, in conjunction with political signals to Washington and Seoul, such heightened activities could be expected to caution unilateral CFC actions. But they would also highlight the possibility (indeed, the necessity) of far more intensive trilateral interactions, so as to ensure that the United States, ROK, and China fully explore how an endgame scenario might be managed without triggering the possibilities of a much larger conflict.

## POTENTIAL INDICATORS

The analytic challenge in this scenario is to determine the circumstances and conditions in the DPRK, and how these would affect either the calculations of a successor regime or the response options of surrounding powers. Evaluating whether North Korea is on the "verge" or "brink" of collapse is by no means easy, since a weakened regime or state could persist for a long time. Conversely, a regime that seems to be fairly intact, despite political and economic problems, could collapse with little advance warning. But understanding Chinese policy calculations in this context would be equally crucial to shaping U.S. and ROK actions.

### Political Indicators

- Foreign policy retrenchment, including widespread recalls of North Korean officials posted abroad.

- Increased Chinese media coverage of instability in the DPRK.

- Increased communication and interaction between Chinese and North Korean leaders.

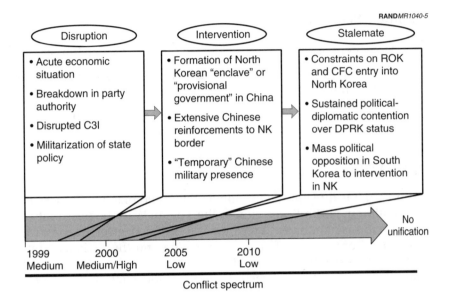

Figure 5—Disequilibrium and Intervention

- Enhanced Chinese communication with U.S., ROK leaderships, possibly including initiatives to U.S., ROK military officials.

## Socioeconomic Indicators

- Increasing refugee flows into China, the Russian Far East, and South Korea.

- Effective governmental control is limited to major urban areas.

- Breakdown of internal passport system.

- Surge in black-market activities.

- Internal economic transactions increasingly limited to hard currencies or barter.

## Military-Security Indicators

- Movement of key PLA units closer to the Sino-Korean border.

- Increased interactions between senior KPA officers and counterparts in the PLA.

- Increased preparations in northeast China for surge in refugees, humanitarian assistance overseen by PLA units.

## VARIATIONS

Although it is difficult to envision an overt and massive Chinese intervention in North Korea akin to the Korean War, the possibility of certain forms of intervention cannot be excluded, given the past role of North Korea as a buffer zone for China and the socioeconomic implications of a highly unstable North Korea, such as a massive influx of refugees into northeastern China. Under such circumstances, the Chinese might opt to deploy security forces across the border, both as an internal control measure and to channel and constrain the more extreme possibilities that could result from North Korean implosion. This said, China would want its actions to be purposeful and even decisive: a protracted, inconclusive situation does not serve Chinese interests. If North Korea remains unstable, Beijing would for a time seek to stabilize it through food and energy shipments, and to control any surge in refugee flows into China. But Beijing has no incentive to take on an open-ended commitment. If North Korea were to rely in ever greater degree on Chinese support, Beijing might decide that a collapse—followed by absorption by the South—is a preferable alternative.

If China decided against a direct intervention, it would nonetheless seek to ensure that any U.S. forces deployed in Korea after unification would remain below the 38th parallel, and that major U.S. strategic assets were not maintained on the peninsula. Alternatively, China could seek to coax South Korea into signing a friendship treaty in return for China's tacit support for unification under ROK auspices, while seeking to limit the scope of future ROK-U.S. security collaboration.

All permutations of this scenario highlight the decisive role that China could assume under conditions of a gravely weakened North.

China has both the capabilities and political-security equities to shape—quite possibly in decisive ways—the ultimate outcome, and few if any incentives to remain passive. These judgments underscore both the critical need to analyze the full spectrum of potential Chinese actions and response options, and the need of the United States and ROK to heighten communication with Beijing at all relevant levels.

# Chapter Seven

# POSTUNIFICATION DYNAMICS AND THEIR
# REGIONAL IMPLICATIONS

For the first time in a half century, there is a distinct possibility of ap-preciable change in inter-Korean dynamics. Should this change result in unification, it would mark a major turning point in postwar Northeast Asia. But unification, however it might ultimately tran-spire, raises a host of unresolved strategic issues: the scale and char-acter of the postunification transition process in the North; the polit-ical arrangements that would govern a unified Korean state; the strategic orientation and policies of the new government; the eco-nomic priorities and policies it would undertake; the composition of a postunification military establishment; and the future of the U.S.-ROK alliance.

These issues and many related questions will undoubtedly pre-occupy Korean and American policymakers and analysts for many years to come. But the "how" of the unification, not the "if" or "when," still represents the most immediate and pressing challenge. The ultimate outcomes in the North—in essence, the results and aftereffects of any endgame scenario—will determine whether a uni-fied Korea is able to move forward in a coherent way to shape its regional strategies and policies, or whether future leaders will be indefinitely preoccupied by the problems of peninsular transition. On balance, it seems highly unlikely that Korean unification will un-fold in a predictable or conflict-free manner. The stakes, risks, and potential for "messy" outcomes seem very high. These considera-tions—and the absence of any broadly shared security understand-ings and arrangements among the powers of Northeast Asia for the postunification era—argue for care and caution in approaching Ko-rea's future. Indeed, these uncertainties and risks seem likely to sustain support within Korea for a close political-military alliance with the United States, even as a unified government simultaneously hopes to define a credible relationship with the major powers that abut the peninsula in all directions.

The central challenge in conceptualizing future scenarios on the Korean peninsula is the disparity between the ultimate objective and the means to achieve it. From the perspective of South Korea, the desired outcome is the ultimate creation of a unified, democratic, and internationalist Korea. To the degree that the United States has been intimately linked with South Korea since its creation, it appears to share this overriding objective. But as events unfold on the peninsula, it remains to be seen whether the ROK and the United States will achieve full agreement on this fundamental goal. This is not to suggest that the United States has a hidden agenda on the peninsula's future, only that the respective roles and contributions of the two countries in the unification process remain to be determined. This is an issue with major and lasting consequences for both countries, and the convergence of U.S. and ROK objectives cannot be taken for granted.

Given geopolitical realities, the strategic calculations of Japan, China, and Russia are necessarily different (and very likely more ambivalent) than those of the United States. Each would need to confront the reality of a unified peninsula, all in the context of their complex historical legacies in 20th-century Korea as well as their prospective involvement in a unified Korea's future development. None has an incentive to see disorder or instability, either during the transition process or in the aftermath of unification. But their respective equities and capabilities to shape a preferred peninsular outcome clearly vary. Though this issue has not been a central focus of this report, a few broad observations seem appropriate.

Given Japan's extensive political and economic linkages with the South and its strategic interdependence with Korea in the context of their respective bilateral security ties with the United States, the prospects for a credible and complementary relationship with a unified Korea seem fairly promising, though far from guaranteed. A degree of distance and wariness is certain to persist, both against the overlay of Japan's past occupation and colonization of Korea; the prospect of a larger strategic or maritime rivalry also cannot be precluded.  This said, there seems ample incentive for both leaderships to pursue in earnest an ongoing consultative relationship in the next century; some of the foundations of these possibilities appear increasingly in place.[1]  Should the peninsula unify, it is not unreasonable to anticipate a substantial Japanese economic and financial role in the rebuilding of the North, though much will depend on the circumstances and needs that would be operative at that time.  And, though both states very likely prefer the maintenance of separate bilateral security alliances with the United States, the prospect of increasing Korean-Japanese defense collaboration also seems credible, with the specific form of this collaboration yet to be determined.

For China, a unified Korean state would constitute an inescapable reality, given the long Sino-Korean border.  For good measure, the presence of a substantial Korean minority population in northeastern China guarantees significant societal, economic, and family interactions.  (Indeed, this contact has increased markedly in the context of North Korea's present vulnerabilities, with private trading activity and North Korean forays into China for food at much higher levels than in the past.)  The Chinese (both before and after unification) will have ample reason to forestall major instability in the North.  A preferred outcome would be one where any instability can be contained within the North's borders, but (as discussed earlier) the Chinese are very likely to hedge against these possibilities, should signs of instability mount.  Whether Chinese actions prior to unification might have longer-term strategic consequences (i.e., whether the Chinese opt to deploy substantial forces in areas contiguous to the peninsula on an extended basis) is necessarily conjectural, though on balance unlikely.

The larger strategic issue for China in the postunification era is the future character and terms of the U.S.-ROK alliance, and the purposes and extent of a continued U.S. military presence on the peninsula following unification.  These issues will, in turn, be contingent on the character and consequences of the unification process, the future evolution of the U.S.-China political and security relationship, and China's capacity to shape strategic and political understandings

---

[1]See, for example, the outcomes and statements of the October 1998 summit between President Kim Dae Jung and Japanese Prime Minister Keizo Obuchi, as reported in *Korea Newsreview,* October 10, 1998, pp. 4–6.

with a unified Korean government.  These questions, while pivotal to longer-term peninsular and regional futures, necessarily take us somewhat beyond the domain of this study.  But they clearly warrant detailed appraisal.

As noted previously, Russia remains marginalized in the current dynamics on the peninsula.  A stable North (either a recovering state or one that has been amalgamated under a unified government) could very likely open the door to Russian involvement in an array of infrastructural projects (e.g., in energy development and resource exploitation).  Still, Russia's larger prospects on the peninsula will very likely depend more on its own political and economic evolution than on Korean developments per se.  Over the longer run, as Russia seeks to reestablish its credibility as a major power in East Asia, political, economic, and security opportunities could well arise, but at present these prospects still seem severely constrained.  This said, Russia will seek to find ways to legitimate a longer-term role in peninsular affairs; the fact alone of a common border (albeit a small one) provides one of the building blocks.  But in comparative terms, Japan and China will have more capability than Russia to shape longer-term peninsular outcomes.

## ASSESSING A UNIFIED KOREA'S INTERESTS

Although it is virtually impossible to forecast when Korea will be unified, we are assuming that it will ultimately be what is termed a "Seoul-centered" unification.  To forecast the prospective characteristics of this new entity requires an assessment of Korea's regional role.  As frequently noted, Korea is unique in that the interests of the four major powers—the United States, China, Japan, and Russia—converge on the peninsula.  From a strategic perspective, Korea stands between Japan and China and either supports or hinders the interactions among China, the Russian Far East, and Japan.  Any major reordering of the regional balance of power would therefore depend on the disposition of Korea.  A unified Korea's strategic value is less as a peer of the major powers, and more as a regional power that could negate the actions of one or more states or, by virtue of its strategic alignment, help shape regional power alignments.  As much as Korea has to calculate the interests of its neighbors in this process, so too do Korea's neighbors.

This strategic linkage between the Korean peninsula and the major powers will persist and very likely be enhanced after unification. Thus, how a unified Korea can contribute to a more stable balance becomes a critical question. A unified Korea could explore three possible security options:    (1) autonomy, (2) alliance, or (3) neutrality. Autonomy could be further disaggregated into nuclear and nonnuclear autonomy. Alliance would entail a strategic relationship with one of the four major powers in order to guarantee or at least significantly enhance Korean security. This could involve the stationing of forces or other arrangements that would call for a close military relationship, but without the deployment of foreign forces. Finally, variations of a neutral Korea could be considered. If the regional powers were to guarantee Korean neutrality, it might have no formal security treaty with any of the four powers.

Each of these options (though necessarily conjectural at present) entails opportunities but also varying costs, both political and economic. If a unified Korea chooses the nuclear option, for example, there would be immediate repercussions and counteractions by the regional powers. A nuclear option would also subject the U.S.-ROK alliance to a profound crisis. Japan would be motivated to pursue larger strategic options, and China could target its nuclear missiles against Korea. Thus, from virtually every perspective, a unified Korea with a declared nuclear capability would lead to a serious deterioration in regional stability, greatly fueling latent strategic rivalries.

At the other extreme, neutrality could be considered, but this would also be very likely to undermine regional stability. Any move made by a neutral Korea could be perceived as favoring one or more of the major powers. Korea is not Switzerland. It cannot simply ignore the fact that the interests of the four major powers are engaged on the peninsula. Neutrality could therefore increase rather than decrease major power competition over Korea, and perturb what is likely to prove a complex, very difficult unification and national integration process.

Thus, comprehensive security planning, ranging from foreign policy guidelines to long-term force modernization goals, will become critical barometers by which to judge the security directions of a unified Korea. The security strategy of a unified Korea has to be transparent, particularly as it pertains to weapons of mass destruction. For reasons noted above, how a unified Korea opts to address the nuclear question could well prove decisive for the regional powers and for regional strategic stability as a whole.

Even with a likely downturn in the growth rate immediately following unification and enormous unification investments (figures range from a low of $250 billion in government expenditure to a high of $3 trillion in total investment), a unified Korea ten years after unification would have a population of over 80 million and, potentially, an economy in which a measure of stabilization and national integration had been realized.[2] (If unification results from military conflict, however, this estimate would need to be recalibrated.) Although it will always be small compared to the major powers, a unified Korea would have significant capabilities and substantial international ties. All the international organizations and regimes to which the South belongs today—United Nations, WTO, OECD, APEC, World Bank, IMF, NPT, and the IAEA, among others—would transfer automatically to a unified Korea.

## KOREA'S REGIONAL ROLE AFTER UNIFICATION

What role could a unified Korea play?[3] In the security arena, the most important issue from a U.S. perspective is whether a unified Korea will retain its security alliance with the United States, the basis on which such an alliance would be maintained, and the composition of postunification U.S. force deployments on the peninsula. Clearly, many of these questions cannot be answered until after the formation of a unified Korean government and follow-on bilateral discussions. From the perspective of the United States, however, the preferred outcome would be a Korean security strategy premised on a series of concentric circles. At its core, Korea would retain an alliance with the United States, though with a different composition of forces if the two governments agree to the continued deployment of

---

[2]The analyses of the costs and benefits of unification are highly variable, reflecting differing assumptions, scenarios, and potential consequences. For a useful overview and some possible projections, see Marcus Noland, Sherman Robinson, and Li-gang Liu, "The Costs and Benefits of Korean Unification—Alternate Scenarios," *Asian Survey*, Vol. 38, No. 8, August 1998, p. 801–814.

[3]For an extended analysis, see Robert Dujarric, Changsu Kim, and Elizabeth A. Stanley, *Korea: Security Pivot in Northeast Asia* (Indianapolis: Hudson Institute, 1998).

U.S. forces following unification. A unified Korea would mean that the United States would have to articulate a new strategic rationale to retain some military presence on the Korean peninsula after unification. In the absence of a North Korean threat, the roles and missions of the Army in Korea would have to be retailored to meet postunification requirements. A drawdown is likely, akin to the downsizing of Army personnel in Germany after unification in 1990. But Korea is the only location on the Asian mainland where the United States retains a military presence. This basic strategic utility of the Korean peninsula could be preserved after unification, though the configuration and character of U.S. forces would change markedly.

Korea's future political, security, and economic ties with Japan will also play an important role in shaping longer-term security dynamics in Northeast Asia. As noted earlier, the checkered history between Korea and Japan rules out any formal military alliance, although the two countries are indirectly linked by their respective alliances with the United States. Some in South Korea argue that an increasingly powerful Japan will emerge ultimately as a potential adversary, particularly after Korean unification. Conversely, there are those in Japan who maintain that a unified Korea would be much more nationalistic and show a growing antipathy toward Japan. Notwithstanding these views, both sides will lose if they target each other as potential adversaries. For a unified Korea, the worst possible strategic outcome would be fractured ties with Japan just as it prepares to launch a major reconstruction effort. For Japan, forging a new partnership with a unified Korea would contribute vitally to its acceptance as a great power in East Asia.

Even if a unified Korea retains a core relationship with the United States and Japan, its ties with China will also expand over time. A shared border, greater economic exchange, and a closer political relationship all point to broader and deeper engagement with China. Indeed, seen from a historical perspective, the absence of formal relations between South Korea and China from 1949 until 1992 was an aberration rather than the norm. Some have argued that a unified Korea that is more nationalistic and perhaps more prone to anti-Americanism may "tilt" toward China in an effort to "preaccommodate" its position. While there is no doubt about the benefits of a stable and mutually beneficial relationship with China, it would not be in the interests of a unified Korea to become hostage to Chinese interests or strategies.  Historically, though Korea appeared to benefit from a security guarantee from China, the costs often proved prohibitive.

Finally, ties with Russia will depend on the outcome of Russia's long-term transformation.  If Russia continues on its reformist path, economic ties are likely to increase.  Energy supplies from Siberia or from Central Asia could play an increasingly important role in determining future Korean-Russian relations.

In the economic realm, a unified Korea's trade relations are likely to focus respectively on China, the United States, Japan, emerging markets in the developing world, and the European Union.  But for the Korean economy not to be dominated by China or Japan, the country must diversify its trade relations, devote much larger resources to research and development, enhance its technology base, and improve productivity.  Systematic but far-reaching deregulation also stands out as a major prerequisite if the Korean economy is to remain competitive in the years ahead.  This is particularly true in relation to the resources that would have to be committed to rebuilding the North's economy after unification.  One major economic asset that differentiates Korea from other emerging markets is its heavy industrial base.  Increased competition from the newly industrialized economies and China has placed new pressures on the Korean economy.  However, in considering the longer-term prospects for the Korean economy, particularly after unification, South Korea's strengths in such areas as shipbuilding, heavy machinery, chemicals, automobiles, and steel could become important catalysts for longer-term dynamism and growth.

In summary, despite lingering concerns about the strategic directions of a unified Korea—ranging from the potential for a nuclear-armed Korea to one allied with China—none of the more pessimistic scenarios is likely to materialize.  Over the last hundred years, wars have been fought on the Korean peninsula involving each of the four major powers.  Twice over the last century, events in the peninsula resulted in a significant power shift in the region.  Japan emerged as the dominant regional power after removing Chinese and Russian influence from Korea.  Some five decades later, the outbreak of the Korean War led to the hardening of the Cold War in East Asia as well as Europe.  At the end of the 20th century, transformations in Korea could yet again affect the regional equilibrium.  For the major powers, a unified Korea that builds rather than threatens stability will be a major strategic asset.  Once the peninsula is unified, its strategic value may lie in its role as a conduit between the great powers and not as a buffer zone or pivot.  For Korea, unification potentially opens the door for a fully realized relationship with all of its more powerful neighbors.

# Chapter Eight

# IMPLICATIONS FOR THE ARMY

For nearly five decades, the United States has maintained a close defense relationship with the ROK, symbolized by a mutual security treaty and the forward deployment of U.S. forces in South Korea. Among the four scenarios analyzed in this study, the Army is most familiar with the conflict scenario, since it has prepared for this contingency for decades, adapting and enhancing its response options in relation to changes in North Korean strategy and capabilities. As argued throughout this report, however, developments in the North could result in outcomes much different from the worst-case contingency (i.e., a full-scale invasion of the ROK). For example, the Army may have to cope with a range of outcomes that confound capabilities-based planning, including actions to cope with a "hollowed-out North Korea" or the deployment of military forces north of the 38th parallel following a North Korean collapse. Some of these potential challenges are noted below.

## FLEXIBLE ROLES AND MISSIONS

The growing uncertainties and potential indeterminacy of political-military outcomes on the peninsula indicate that the Army may well have to assume very different roles and missions, potentially on a fairly abrupt basis. In the event of a rapid North Korean collapse, and assuming that the ROK successfully establishes political authority throughout the North, U.S. Army and ROK units attached to CFC (and other units that would augment these forces) would have to perform a much broader range of missions. Humanitarian assistance, various types of peace operations, dismantling and management of weapons of mass destruction (WMD), and assisting the demobilization of the North Korean armed forces are among the responsibilities that the Army could assume, including joint operations with the ROK forces.  If instability persists in North Korea but without collapse, the Army would have to enhance deterrence capabilities, given that a weakened but more unstable North would be an ongoing concern for ROK and U.S. security planners.

## NEW INTELLIGENCE DEMANDS

The Army also needs to enhance its intelligence-collection and analysis capabilities across a broader spectrum of issues.  Demand for intelligence will increase significantly if North Korea lies on the brink of a collapse or if China seems poised to take actions, including a further augmentation of economic and humanitarian assistance and redeployments of selected military units toward the Chinese–North Korean border.  If the Kim Jong Il regime is replaced by a party-military junta, Army intelligence would face the task of analyzing the overall military capabilities of the new regime, the level of its military preparedness (such as readiness levels of operational maneuver groups), and the degree of control over North Korean military assets, especially WMD assets.  In addition, data collection and assessment of Chinese–North Korean political, military, and economic relations would loom as a major challenge.  Even under current circumstances, these issues all represent pressing analytic and intelligence requirements.

## OPERATIONAL REQUIREMENTS

The Army will also face new operational requirements as Korea moves toward unification, particularly if the reconstruction of the North's economy and infrastructure and integration of the peninsula into a single political entity become a reality.  Rather than a seamless unification process, these circumstances will involve unprecedented (and potentially unanticipated) problems, requiring a very different mix of Army capabilities than the present one.  These changes in responsibility and force mix will require adaptation at all levels, including operational control arrangements, logistical and training requirements, and rules of engagement for the ample gray zone between major theater war and humanitarian and peacekeeping operations.

Major challenges, potentially extending to various forms of multilateral collaboration, are faced in two additional areas: dismantlement of North Korean WMD capabilities and interactions with Chinese officials and military personnel. Control over and disposition of WMD assets is not necessarily an Army responsibility as such, though the Army would find itself involved in this process, in either a benign or a more threatening scenario. But a wide array of unprecedented bilateral and multilateral relationships may have to be implemented in this area, prospectively involving the United States and China; the United States, Russia, and China; or the United States, ROK, and IAEA. It seems very likely that Army assets will be called upon in such scenarios.

Establishing closer linkages and lines of communication with China (including at a military-to-military level) could also emerge as a pressing priority. In view of the growing possibility of instability and the responses this could trigger by the United States, ROK, and China, it seems crucial that these linkages be in place before any full-scale crisis erupts on the peninsula. Absent such means of communication, there would be incentives for unilateral action on all sides that could trigger highly adverse responses. If the risks of a larger conflict on the peninsula are to be managed, this cannot be achieved without effective ties with China, including its military leadership and (quite possibly) senior People's Liberation Army commanders in northeastern China.

## INTEGRATION AND PEACEFUL UNIFICATION

For the Army, peaceful unification would pose few appreciable military risks. Major strategic issues, such as the desirability of maintaining U.S. military assets on the Korean peninsula after unification, would have to be closely discussed during the process of political negotiations between the two Koreas. The four-party talks venue might afford a format for exploration of longer-term security arrangements on the peninsula. Alternatively, postunification security planning could be handled through U.S.-ROK channels. Though the possibility seems remote, termination of extant treaty relationships and withdrawal of the U.S. military presence on the peninsula after unification represent potential options under some circumstances. But peaceful unification would furnish the Army ample lead time to conceptualize postunification presence modalities, assuming that the United States and a unified Korea see a strategic need to maintain a U.S. military presence on the peninsula.

## COLLAPSE AND ABSORPTION

The collapse scenario entails significant operational challenges for defense planners in the United States and the ROK. While CFC has trained for a variety of contingencies, a sudden collapse of the North Korean regime or even the dissolution of the DPRK would imply entirely new roles and missions for CFC and other components of U.S. forces earmarked for South Korea. Capabilities-based planning and training could be of limited value in coping with an imminent or actual regime or state collapse in the North. However, CFC must retain in place the needed capabilities to maintain an effective deterrence posture and, should deterrence fail, initiate effective military responses.

If the Kim Jong Il regime is ousted in a military coup or by other means and a successor regime is in place, the pivotal strategic issue would be to determine that regime's political and military objectives, the type of military policies it is likely to pursue, and the level of threat it poses to the ROK. But should the successor regime prove unable to maintain effective control over the armed forces, resulting in accidental escalation or deliberate military strikes by units no longer under effective command and control, CFC would face a crucial operational challenge. If the command, control, communications, and intelligence system ($C^3I$) of the KPA begins to break down, CFC would need to assess the vulnerability as well as lethality of key KPA units and to formulate credible response options for such a threat.

If a regime collapse is followed by a state collapse, CFC would confront a range of new military requirements. First, assuming that negotiations would be conducted between some elements of the KPA or an ad hoc leadership group, a priority goal would be to ensure internal stability within North Korea and to avoid any spillover of instability into the South. If internal stability is not maintained, ROK forces could undertake peace operations within North Korea, but such a move presumes that ROK forces would be able to enter North Korean territory without significant military resistance. CFC would also need to verify whether the KPA retained effective control over key WMD locations, including ballistic missile sites, chemical or biological weapons depots and plants, and nuclear facilities. Potential demobilization of the KPA and the dismantling of its major hardware and weapon systems would require major efforts by CFC units, possibly augmented by additional forces deployed to the peninsula. Any military activities in the northern half of Korea, however, would be predicated on prior political agreement reached among the relevant parties, including China.

## UNIFICATION THROUGH CONFLICT

There are three major operational implications under the conflict scenario. First, capabilities-based planning would play a central role in managing any major hostilities on the Korean peninsula. Second, CFC would need to prepare a full range of military options that carry the threat of escalation. For example, if the DPRK launches a limited military attack on a South Korean military base near the DMZ, how would CFC respond? Or if North Korea launches one or two Scud missiles at a U.S. Air Force base in South Korea, would CFC engage in military actions that would guarantee a significant expansion of the conflict? Third, what if the KPA launches a particular military action that turns out to be "accidental" in nature? If one assumes that political and social chaos prevails in North Korea, the threat of accidental use of force (or actions that North Korea asserts are accidental) increases substantially. These potential developments suggest that future conflict scenarios on the Korean peninsula need to be assessed in relation to much less predictable decisionmaking contexts. This issue warrants careful consideration and discussion with Japan as well as the ROK.

## DISEQUILIBRIUM AND POTENTIAL EXTERNAL INTERVENTION

The major analytical challenges under a disequilibrium scenario are to fully assess the degree of domestic stability in North Korea; to posit conditions under which the Chinese might choose to intervene, and the character of this intervention; and to determine how such an intervention or "virtual intervention" would influence U.S. and ROK political and military objectives. Augmentation of CFC capabilities also warrants ample attention in this context, especially if a "hollowed-out North Korea" condition persists over a considerable period. The Army would require ample lead time to upgrade its capabilities in preparation for a range of operations that it may need to undertake. Should signs of imminent or virtual Chinese intervention mount, there would be an imperative need for trilateral discussions among the United States, ROK, and China, thereby seeking to limit the risks of a direct military clash on the peninsula and more credibly determine Chinese strategic objectives.

The scope and consequences of these issues clearly indicate the need for focused and much-enhanced attention at a policymaking level and with respect to future U.S. Army operations in Korea. Though a relatively painless stabilization process on the peninsula (up to and including unification) is devoutly to be wished, we see little prospect of such a benign outcome. It is thus incumbent on the Army to prepare for a future that entails numerous risks, dangers, and negative consequences, as these seem ever more possible.